HC
256.5
.J59
1985

Jones, Aubrey, 1911-

Britain's economy

DATE			

BRITAIN'S ECONOMY

The roots of stagnation

AUBREY JONES

Fellow Commoner, Churchill College, Cambridge

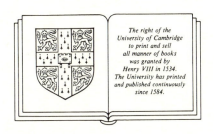

CAMBRIDGE UNIVERSITY PRESS

Cambridge
London   New York   New Rochelle
Melbourne   Sydney

Published by the Press Syndicate of the University of Cambridge
The Pitt Building, Trumpington Street, Cambridge CB2 1RP
32 East 57th Street, New York, NY 10022, USA
10 Stamford Road, Oakleigh, Melbourne 3166, Australia

First published 1985

Printed in Great Britain at the University Press, Cambridge

British Library cataloguing in publication data

Jones, Aubrey, *1911–*
Britains economy: the roots of stagnation.
1. Great Britain – Economic conditions – 1945–
I. Title
330.941′0858   HC256.6

Library of Congress cataloguing in publication data

Jones, Aubrey, 1911–
Britain's economy.
Bibliography: p.
Includes index.
1. Great Britain – Economic conditions – 1945–
2. Unemployment – Great Britain – Effect of inflation on.
3. Stagnation (Economics) I. Title.
HC256.6.J64 1985   330.941′0858   85–9649

ISBN 0 521 30816 X

CONTENTS

v

In Memoriam
T.B.

ACKNOWLEDGEMENTS

The purpose of this book is to present reflections on the British economic problem as I have seen it in my own experience. The book is therefore in part autobiographical, the autobiographical sections forming in turn the foundation on which rest my conclusions about the United Kingdom.

That I was able to write the book was due in the main to Professor Sir William Hawthorne who invited me to renew an earlier experience and spend some time at Churchill College, Cambridge. He and Professor H. A. Turner acted there as my guides and mentors. Churchill College is rich in its archives, and I am greatly indebted to Miss Marion Stewart, the archivist, for guiding me through labyrinthine ways. I owe a similar debt to Dr Raspin, who led me through the oral archives of the British Library of Political and Economic Science. By extension I have to thank those who have allowed me to quote from papers lodged there. A short spell at the Brookings Institution in Washington, DC, financed by the Sloan Foundation, proved invaluable. The same was true of a short stay in Paris, made possible by the Nuffield Foundation.

Thanks are also due to the various parts of Government which allowed me to re-read the papers which I was entitled to see – the Cabinet Office, and the Departments of Energy, Defence and Employment. Unfortunately, the Department of Trade and Industry was unable to trace papers relating to my time as Minister of Supply.

Much help was received from friends who either gave me of their time or, alternatively, read parts of the script. I should like to mention Sir Alan Cottrell, Professor Richard Eden, Professor Brian Reddaway and Professor J. E. Meade, at Cambridge; Mr Roger Opie and Mr Derek Robinson at Oxford; Mr Peter Maunder and Mr Michael Fleming at Loughborough University; Sir Walter Marshall of the Central Elec-

tricity Generating Board and Dr Lewis Roberts and his team at the
Harwell Research Establishment of the Atomic Energy Authority.

The typing, an art which I have forgotten, was done by Miss Kay
Dunlop, whose patience was beyond words.

It would be nice to end on an optimistic note a book about a relative
decline which is beyond dispute. Alas, I do not believe in immediate
miracles and the trends as I see them do not allow me to strike the note
which I would wish.

A.J.

ABBREVIATIONS

ACARD	Advisory Council for Applied Research and Development
AEA	Atomic Energy Authority
AGR	Advanced Gas Cooled Reactor
ANVAR	Agence Nationale pour la Valorisation de la Recherche
BEA	British European Airways
BEA	British Electricity Authority
BMFT	Bundesministerium für Forschung und Technologie
BOAC	British Overseas Airways Corporation
CBI	Confederation of British Industry
CEA	Central Electricity Authority
CEGB	Central Electricity Generating Board
CIM	Commission for Industry and Manpower
DEA	Department of Economic Affairs
EEC	European Economic Community
FBI	Federation of British Industry
IMF	International Monetary Fund
mbd	million barrels a day
mtce	million tons of coal equivalent
NBPI	National Board for Prices and Incomes
NEB	National Enterprise Board
NEDO	National Economic Development Office
NRDC	National Research and Development Corporation
NUM	National Union of Mineworkers
OECD	Organisation for Economic Co-operation and Development
OEEC	Organisation for European Economic Co-operation
OPEC	Organisation of Petroleum Exporting Countries
PWR	Pressurised Water Reactor
RAF	Royal Air Force
R and D	Research and Development
TUC	Trades Union Congress

1

THE FIRST GLIMPSE

Number 6, Plantation Terrace, Penydarren – between Merthyr Tydfil and Dowlais. That was the house where I was born. It is gone now, demolished. So also is that, of an earlier vintage, of my maternal grandparents, in one of the older origins of the same street. Both were products of the tidal wave of industrialism and cosmopolitanism which in the nineteenth century swept up the valleys of South Wales, leaving islands of Welshness. It was on one of these islands that we lived.

As a family I suppose we cannot have been unprosperous. At any rate some time in the First World War we moved into a larger house, with a bathroom at that, though the toilet was still outside. I remember carting some of our possessions through the blacked-out night. The move must have been the result of my father's rise up the ladder. Schooled by my mother in English, he graduated from being a miner into becoming a 'fireman' or, to use the formal expression, a deputy. The name 'fireman' seems to go back to the eighteenth century, when, in advance of the main body of miners, he entered the pit carrying in a heavily swathed arm a flare with which to test along the roof for gas, and, if found, set it alight. In short, he was a safety officer.

When the war was over the need to secure the mine for safety continued. During the strikes of the twenties in particular, the mine had to be kept clear of water. On those occasions my father used to take me with him. The pickets, knowing what we were about, peacefully let us through. I have therefore no congenital dislike of pickets. On the whole then things were not too bad.

The shadows, however, soon began to lengthen. In the High Street one day I read that the Castle Pit, Troedyrhiw, was to be closed. An uncle, who lived with us, worked there. He never worked again. The remainder of his life he spent sitting morosely over the fire and intermittently coughing.

A little later my father contracted pneumoconiosis, a disease of the

1

lungs caused by coal dust. Further work underground was impossible and a job had to be sought aloft. He found it as a labourer in the local steel works. He was demolishing one of the blast furnaces when King Edward VIII visited South Wales. My father never worked again. I believe that, an active man, he died of sheer frustration.

The first flicker of prosperity then proved false. Only since have I come to realise that I was born the citizen of a country in relative decline; in the years that remain to me the relative may be turning into the absolute.

Carlo M. Cippola has opined that 'all cases of decline turn out eventually to be cases of relative decline', except where societies actually die out.[1] The justification of the view that the relative British decline may be turning into an absolute decline rests on the extent of the destruction caused by the depression of the late 1970s and early 1980s, the destruction of physical equipment and, through unemployment, the demoralisation of human beings. The destruction has been such that it is very difficult, certainly in this century, to envisage its eventual repair – that is, the rise of enough new equipment or new activities to restore dignity to the unemployed.

Various dates have been put to the beginning of the relative decline – from 1840 to 1870. Certainly the apogee was marked by the Crystal Palace Exhibition of 1851,[2] though there had been earlier indications of successful emulation by other countries, acting under state guidance. The Exhibition itself was quickly followed by the deaths of the great engineers of the first half of the nineteenth century – Brunel, Robert Stephenson and Joseph Locke. And 'By the last third of the century . . . Britain no longer stood alone as the workshop of the world.'[3] Instead she 'basked in the complacency of the sunset of economic hegemoney.'[4]

For myself I choose two dates as significant – 1900 and 1950. The year 1900 I choose because it was in that year that Gross Domestic Product per man in the United States overtook that in the United Kingdom.[5] It was also a decade or so before my birth. The year 1950 I choose because it was then that I entered the House of Commons, and

[1]   Carlo M. Cippola, ed., *The Economic Decline of Empires*, Methuen, London, 1970.
[2]   David S. Landes, *The Unbound Prometheus*, Cambridge University Press, 1969.
[3]   Ibid., p. 239.   [4]   Ibid., p. 336.
[5]   See R. C. O. Matthews, C. H. Feinstein and J. C. Odling-Smee, *British Economic Growth 1856–1973*, Stanford University Press, 1982.

started to deepen my glimpse. It was also the year which the United Kingdom began to be overtaken by France and Germany; in terms of G.D.P. per head she had been overtaken by both countries by 1960; by Italy by 1970, and by Japan in the late 1970s. The comparison with Germany is especially striking. In 1950 labour productivity in British manufacturing industry was 31 per cent above that in German industry; by 1959 productivity in German industry equalled that in British industry; but by 1970 productivity in German industry was 23 per cent above that in Britain.[6] My entire life therefore seems destined to have been spent in the service of a country in decline. Is there anything even at this late stage which can be done to retrieve the decline? The answer depends on the causes to which one ascribes the decline.

The causes put forward range from those which, at one extreme, put the decline beyond any retrieval to those which, at the other, offer some ray of hope.

At the pessimistic end there stands Mr Martin J. Wiener, who sees the budding industrialist absorbed by the prevailing agricultural aristocracy.[7] 'Through the mechanism of social absorption, the zeal for work, inventiveness, material production and money making gave way within the capitalist class to the more aristrocratic interests of cultivated style, the pursuit of leisure and political service.'[8] The industrialist, in short, became 'gentrified', and the attractiveness of the City of London over industry lay in the closer approximation to the ideal of the 'gentry'.

Nor was it only the industrialist who fell captive to the spell of the territorial squire. There were also the poets and the artists. William Morris, for example, hoped to see England 'become again the fair green garden of Northern Europe'.[9]

Finally, according to Mr Wiener, the gentlemanly idea has retained its power up to contemporary times. He quotes Sir John Hanbury-Williams, under whom I served when he was chairman of Courtaulds, as saying to the annual general meeting of shareholders in 1952: 'There has been a Gentleman's Club atmosphere in the Board Room, and I believe it true to say that over the years this has spread to all

---

[6]   S. J. Prais, *Productivity and Industrial Structure*, Cambridge University Press, 1981.

[7]   Martin J. Wiener, *English Culture and the Decline of The Industrial Spirit, 1850–1890*, Cambridge University Press, 1981.

[8]   Ibid., p. 13.   [9]   Ibid.

departments of our business. It is, in fact, part of the goodwill of the company which we must safeguard.'[10]

If indeed the British economic problem is a problem of culture, it is not easy to see what can be done about it. If the explanation is sound, we have no option but to live with our fate. But is it sound? Why, among all the European countries which moved at different stages and different paces from an agricultural to an industrial society, did Britain alone remain attached to the values of the ruling agricultural elite? Perhaps an explanation lies in the generally accepted thought that the Industrial Revolution in Britain was not initiated by merchant–industrial capital; it had been preceded by the commercialisation of the squirearchy's landed interests; the squirearchy thus retained its dominance. The squire was the initial entrepreneur. Nonetheless, there remains something of a conundrum. Even after the passage, in the first half of the nineteenth century, of the Corn Laws which were aimed at favouring the consumer as against the producer, the landed gentry still retained their dominance.

A somewhat, though not entirely, different explanation of the British decline has been expressed by Mr Corelli Barnett.[11] He sees the romantic movement which swept Western Europe in the eighteenth century – and the essence of romanticism was to place feeling above calculation and judgement – as having taken in Britain a peculiarly religious form. The effect was double. First, 'it came to be more and more generally felt by public opinion that moral principle and moral purpose rather than strategy or mere interest alone should be the inspiration of British policy.'[12]

Secondly, and from the economic point of view more important, if economic power can indeed be dissociated from military power, the religious evangelical movement moulded British education. According to Dr Arnold, headmaster of Rugby, 'Christian morality was more important than scientific knowledge: rather than have it [science] the principal thing in my son's mind, I would gladly have him think that the sun went round the earth.'[13]

In vain did Herbert Spencer plead for science as the foundation of education, for the concept of education as having to do with the practical business of life. Some three-quarters of a century later the triumphant

[10] Ibid., pp. 148–9.
[11] Corelli Barnett, *The Collapse of British Power*, Eyre Methuen, London, 1972.
[12] Ibid., pp. 20, 21.   [13] Ibid., p. 25.

creed was expounded by Dr Cyril Norwood, headmaster of Harrow:

> 'in the course of the last hundred years . . . the old ideals have been recaptured. The ideal of chivalry which inspired the Knighthood of medieval days, the ideal of service to the community which inspired the greatest of men who founded schools for their day and for posterity, have been combined in the tradition of English education which holds the field today. It is based upon religion; it relies largely on games and open-air prowess, where these involve corporate effort.'[14]

Mr Barnett appears to come nearer to the mark than Mr Wiener in explaining both the loss of British military might and the simultaneous weakening of British economic strength. But, even though one may go along with his thesis, it is not easy to discern what should now be done about it.

Mr M. W. Kirby perhaps offers some gleam of a remedy.[15] His thesis is that Britain, as the first industrial power, aided by the steady reduction in the costs of ocean-going transport, began to develop a close trading relationship with the primary producing countries of the world. The result was 'to retard the development of more advanced industrial sectors in the British economy.'[16] In other words, Britain's links were with the backward world, not with the newly developing world. Further, overseas investment in raw materials and primary products reinforced the 'over-commitment of the economy to the old-established industries.'[17]

A similar view has been expressed by Sir Henry Phelps-Brown, who cites the slow change in the composition of British exports between the Edwardian era and the inter-war period. This slow adoption of new products was comparable to the performance of Italian industry in the seventeenth century and of Dutch industry and trade in the eighteenth century; it is put forward as the most plausible explanation of the long relative decline in British economic performance.[18] Some evidence to support this view will be adduced later in the book.

The pattern of trading low-value goods to under-developed countries could not conceivably have continued in a world in which every country is intent on industrialising itself. The trading relationship

---

[14] Ibid., p. 27.
[15] M. W. Kirby, *The Decline of British Economic Power since 1870*, Allen and Unwin, London, 1981.   [16] Ibid., p. 16.   [17] Ibid., p. 16.
[18] Sir Henry Phelps-Brown, 'What is the British Predicament?' *Three Banks Review*, December 1977.

with the Commonwealth was beginning to break down before Britain's entry into the European Economic Community, and indeed the fact precipitated entry. Entry may have brought with it its difficulties; the very change was bound to create them. The fact remains that Britain has now to trade with industrialised and industrialising countries. The problem is how to do it successfully.

Yet another hypothesis, not without plausibility, has been advanced by Mancur Olson.[19] His broad argument is that stable societies, societies, that is, which have not for a long period undergone the ravages of war or revolution, when everything is razed to the ground and has to be rebuilt, will develop organisations or coalitions concerned with capturing for themselves as large a proportion of the national product as they can.

Applied to Britain, the hypothesis, it is suggested, explains

> the powerful network of special interest organisations [to be expected] in a country with its record of military security and democratic stability. The number and power of its trade unions need no description. The venerability and power of its professional associations is [sic] also striking . . . Britain also has a strong farmers' organisation and a great many trade associations. In short, with age British society has acquired so many strong organisations and collusions that it suffers from an institutional sclerosis that slows its adaptation to changing circumstances and technologies.[20]

Mr Olson's hypothesis appears to explain why the country which launched the Industrial Revolution seems suddenly to have run out of impulse. Whether, on the other hand, he is wise to apply his hypothesis universally – he uses it to explain the caste system of India and apartheid in South Africa – is another matter. And even his description of the United Kingdom does not ring entirely true. There are coalitions of interests in Japan. But, in contrast with the United Kingdom, Japan 'has grown to be the second biggest western economy precisely by incorporating these features [e.g. oligopolies] which are deplored elsewhere, as integral functioning elements of its system of organised capitalism. It has seen the shape of the future, accepted it, and made it work.'[21] In other words Japanese unions, while nominally fitting into Olson's category of organisations determined to capture for

---

[19] Mancur Olson, *The Rise and Decline of Nations*, Yale University Press, 1982.
[20] Ibid., pp. 77–8.
[21] Ronald Dore, *Flexible Rigidities: Industrial Policy and Structural Adjustments in the Japanese Economy 1970–80*, World Employment Programme Research Paper, p. 264.

themselves as much as they can of the national product, in fact seek to operate in the context of a national consensus. British unions, by contrast, have a preference for individual assertiveness, and as a result are fragmented. It is relevant to note that the late Lord Citrine, when general secretary of the Trades Union Congress, tried to move the unions towards centralised bargaining. He resigned when the General Council of the TUC rejected a proposal of its Organisation Committee that there should be regional TUC offices. The question then which Olson's thesis poses, but which he does not answer, is why coalitions of interest fit into a national consensus in some countries, while in others they remain self-seeking and therefore divided.

A view, starting like Olson's from the premise of stability and maturity in a nation, but without advancing into the elaboration of entrenched self-interested groups, has been put forward by Carlo Cippola.[22] The problem for him is the 'strong conservatism of mature empires.' 'The more a mature empire is proud of its cultural heritage, the more emotionally difficult it is for its people to change to new modes of being and new ways of doing things, under the pressure of external competition and growing difficulties.'

Finally, an economic view of the latest phase of the British decline has been advanced by Sidney Pollard.[23] He sees the immediate cause of the 'one failure in the Western European success story since the war' (p. 14) as lagging investment, and the causes behind the immediate cause as two: first a general attitude of 'concentrating first and foremost on symbolic figures and quantities, like prices, exchange rates and balances of payment, to the neglect of real quantities like goods and services produced and traded' (p. 72); secondly, the Treasury, to which 'Economy in public expenditure is ... its most deeply held conviction' (p. 90). Yet the Treasury is also the formulator of macro-economic policy, and in this capacity it acts ultimately in the same way. 'Here it plays the part of the wastrel, the spendthrift and the unregenerate rake, for ... its standard and systematic method of solving the immediate and 'urgent' problems of the day was to cut investment every time – in other words at the expense of the future' (p. 91). When an alteration in policy has come about, generally on the eve of a General Election, it has taken the form of a boost to consumption. The lag in investment has, as a result, persisted. In so far as Sidney Pollard

[22] Cippola, op. cit.
[23] Sidney Pollard, *The Wasting of the British Economy*, Croom Helm, London, 1982.

has a remedial prescription it is 'a mixed system in which much of the steering and the initiative is taken on by the state, on the French or Japanese model' (p. 189). That happens to be very close to the conclusion reached in the present book.

It is not the purpose of this book to advance, like Mr Olson, a hypothesis of allegedly universal applicability. Nor is it to expound any general explanation of the British predicament. The object rather is to describe the British plight as I have seen it from the standpoint of various positions occupied – back-bench member of the House of Commons, Minister of Fuel and Power, Minister of Supply, chairman of the National Board for Prices and Incomes, member of various industrial boards. I shall try, within the ambit of my experience, to indicate where we have gone wrong, and how perhaps we might do better. I doubt whether there is any one single explanation for our troubles; there are probably several explanations. But we shall see.

2

THE BEGINNINGS OF THATCHERISM

In 1950 I entered the House of Commons. Its composition, at least on the Conservative side, was far different then from now. It still contained captains of industry – Sir Peter Bennett, Oliver Lyttleton (later Lord Chandos). The large-scale industrialist has gone now. His place has been taken by the self-made and smaller-scale business man, rougher and cruder, though still rubbing shoulders with the traditionally large quota of barristers. On the Labour side I doubt whether the composition has changed much. A trade unionist aspires either to become a trade union leader or, if that is beyond his grasp, to enter the House of Commons. Traditionally he cannot be both a trade union leader and a Member of Parliament. There has, of course, been the occasional exception – Ernest Bevin, in the special circumstances of war, and later Mr Frank Cousins. The trade unionist in the House tends therefore to be dominated by the intellectuals, more often than not farther to the Left than he.

As a newcomer I was little conscious of the impotence of individual members and of their imprisonment in the policies of the Chancellor of the Exchequer whom they support or in those of his predecessors. I mention the Chancellor of the Exchequer rather than the Prime Minister because it is to the former rather than the latter that every spending Minister – and which Minister does not spend? – has to defer. Even under the overlordship of Mrs Thatcher that would still be true.

When Labour fell from power in 1951 the first Conservative Chancellor of the Exchequer was Rab Butler. It was loyalty to him which was demanded of me. His name is enshrined in the expression 'Butskellism', implying that he subscribed to the consensus politics of the war-time coalition government and in particular to the commitment to full employment. I have no doubt that Butler wished to maintain full employment; he preferred to swim with the tide rather than against it. But in other respects Butler was no 'Butskellite'. On the contrary one sees under him the early stirrings of an attempt to regulate the economy through the supply of money rather than through the budget, as had been prescribed by Keynes, and the first steps along the road which finally, in 1979, took the Conservative Party to Thatcherism and the abandonment of consensus politics. Butlerism and Thatcherism I would define as attempts to reverse the British decline by a restoration of the conditions believed to have given rise to the Industrial Revolution.

The history needs retelling. A condition of the loan granted to Britain by the United States on the morrow of the Second World War was that the pound sterling should be freely convertible into other currencies (particularly dollars) within twelve months. It was a hard condition, accepted only under duress. Nonetheless it was acted on by Dr Dalton, Labour's first Chancellor, with disastrous results. No sooner was convertibility reintroduced than it had to be suspended again; we simply did not have the dollars.

Roughly five years after the end of the Second World War in 1945 'the British economy had . . . completed its recovery from the effects of the war'.[1] This was true, except for one important fact – Britain was still short of dollars. And her efforts to win dollars were defeated by the programme of rearmament following the outbreak of the Korean war in 1950 – the choice has always been guns, on the one hand, and, on the other, investment and exports. The rearmament programme was begun under Labour, the Chancellor of the Exchequer Hugh Gaitskell, being insistent that priority be given to arms, no matter at what cost to the economy. The Americans gave the impression that they would underwrite any adverse effect of rearmament on the balance of payments, but the implied promise was never kept. To the distraction from exports resulting from rearmament, there was added the burden on building resources arising from the populist promise, at a Conservative Party conference, to build 300,000 houses a year. This was the first instance, in the conservative of all parties, of a mass conference laying down the Government's policy, before the Government had even 'seen the books'.

In the midst of the balance of payments crisis resulting from rearmament and, to a lesser extent, the commitment to build more houses, Butler proceeded once again to make the pound freely convertible into other currencies. The moment could scarcely have been less

[1]   J. C. R. Dow, *The Management of the British Economy 1945–60*, Cambridge University Press, 1965, p. 53.

propitious. It was opposed by both Sir Robert Hall (later Lord Roberthall), the Treasury's economic adviser, and by Sir Edwin (later Lord) Plowden, the Chief Planning Officer.[2] Butler, however, pushed ahead, submitting his proposal to the Cabinet. Why such unaccustomed boldness? The only intellectual reason can have been a belief that a return to nineteenth-century arrangements could alone quicken Britain to life again. The move was akin to that of Winston Churchill in the mid-1920s when the pound sterling was restored to its pre-1914 parity with the dollar. It was as though a return to the past would bring back again the paradise of the past. As Mr J. C. R. Dow has put it: 'The Commonwealth conference that met in London in January 1951 ... treated the achievement of convertibility as a main aim of policy – words which seemed "strangely brave" after the silence that had reigned since the convertibility fiasco five years before ... why such emphasis, when sterling was so weak?'[3]

Why indeed? This was the question asked by the Cabinet, where Butler, as recorded by Lord Birkenhead, was opposed by Lord Cherwell.[4] What has not been recorded is that Butler was also opposed by his Economic Secretary, Sir Arthur (later Lord) Salter. Churchill commented that when both Cherwell and Salter were united in opposition to a project, the project must be flawed. Salter, to whom I was closely attached, was embarrassed at having opposed and defeated his superior Minister.

Accordingly, he expressed a wish to resign. Churchill's answer was that if Salter went to the back benches he would criticise; accordingly Salter was given another post – the head of the dying Ministry of Materials, an unworthy end to a career of great distinction. But Churchill, even in demeaning Salter, also showed his wisdom, a wisdom not displayed by Conservative successors.

Exchange policy was not the only respect in which Butler retreated from Butskellism. He abandoned Labour's practice of promulgating targets, which at least gave one a view of problems looming ahead. And in the spring of 1955, when the economy was booming and an orthodox Keynesian would have raised taxes in order to weaken the pressure of demand, Butler lowered them. 'To a cold eye it may seem that he was relying on monetary policy to work wonders.'[5] He reaped

---

[2] Lord Roberthall, British Oral Archives of Political and Administrative History, British Library of Political and Economic Science.   [3] Dow, op. cit., p. 80.
[4] The Earl of Birkenhead, *The Prof in Two Worlds*, Collins, London, 1961, p. 284.   [5] Dow, op. cit., p. 79.

his bitter reward in the autumn, when the balance of payments was deteriorating and there was a run on sterling. Having, before the election of May 1955, introduced an easy budget, he had now to resort to something tougher. Taxes were raised and public investment was cut. Cast inevitably in the role of changeling and scapegoat, he had to resign.

Butler's lineal descendant, though not his immediate successor, in pushing the Conservative Party further down the road to 'monetarism' was Mr (now Lord) Thorneycroft. His advisers were Lord Robbins and Professor Paish. Lord Robbins had earlier declared that the supreme test of economic policy was the balance of payments and the value of money.[6] These are, in fact, two tests, not one, and they are not necessarily consistent the one with the other. One could inconceivably 'balance' the balance of payments by devaluing the pound, but that would raise prices and lower the value of money. And is one to seek a constant value of money whatever the cost of attainment? As for Professor Paish, he was famous for his prophecy that if unemployment were raised to the rate of 2.5 per cent, inflation would be stilled. How ironical now that unemployment is at a rate of some 13 per cent that earnings per man among the employed should still be rising faster than output per man!

Lord Thorneycroft's 'monetarism' was at its most revealing in his resignation early in 1958. The economy was moving into recession and, accordingly to the Keynesian prescription, required some injection of spending by the Government. Lord Thorneycroft, however, with his other Treasury Ministers, the late Nigel Birch and Mr Enoch Powell, wanted to reduce planned spending on the social services by £50 million – a trifle. At a gathering of officials to which the trio of Ministers explained their view, a then relatively junior official asked them whether they thought they could carry the Cabinet with them. Mr Enoch Powell, who until then had played a relatively quiet role, took it upon himself to reply. 'Unhesitatingly, yes.' Not for the first time Mr Powell was hopelessly wrong. To be fair to Lord Thorneycroft, however, he seems in later years to have modified his views. As an industrialist he was a staunch supporter of the CBI's initiative in the early 1960s in 'freezing' prices.

It is time, however, to return to Rab Butler. As a back-bencher I had no direct contact with him. His influence was rather indirect and bet-

---

[6]   Pollard, *The Wasting of the British Economy*, Croom Helm, London, 1982, p. 41.

rayed itself in the one major reform which I tried to institute in my first five years as a back-bencher. It concerned the denationalisation of road haulage. At the committee stage of the bill I tried to introduce an amendment designed to make possible the sale to the public of 'haulage enterprises' and not just numbers of vehicles. The Labour and Liberal parties supported me. The Junior Minister, by contrast, stone-walled. Since the issue raised was financial, he would clearly have consulted the Treasury. At the Report stage the Minister himself was placatory; he would give the proposal sympathetic consideration.

In the House of Lords he acted. He, or rather his spokesman, put forward an amendment on exactly the lines which I had suggested. True, he implied that the proportion of the total road-haulage business which might be sold in enterprise form might not be all that great. Nonetheless, the principle was conceded.

Back in the Commons, the Opposition was furious. Why had the change been made in the Lords? Why had it not been accepted when first mooted in the Commons? That is the intriguing and indeed significant part of the entire story.

The answer lies in the nature of the House of Commons and in its physical shape: a rectangle on one side of which sit knights in shining armour, and on the other enemies who would destroy them. In this pit every suggestion of help, even from the shining side, is not seen as a proffer of assistance; rather is it viewed as a covert attempt to wreck. All governments are thus warily defensive, even to the point of blinding them to helpful reform.

This impression was borne in on me more vividly when later I was a Minister. I had to answer questions on a Monday. The questions and officials' draft answers to them arrived on my desk on a Friday evening. I dealt with them at home the following morning. Had any questions drawn my attention to some error of omission or commission, there was no time between Friday evening and Monday afternoon to rectify it. The brevity of the interval drove me, against my will, on to the defensive. But then that is the point of the exercise – to defend, not to change. I cannot remember a single question which opened my eyes to a possible new line of policy and which I would have gladly followed. Sadly I conclude that that hallowed hour of the Mother of Parliaments (is she really the mother?) which goes by the name of question time may make for theatre, but it is a drag on any attempt to arrest the national decline. In sum, it is a pointless charade.

When later still, having ceased to be a Minister, I returned to the back benches, I did not find a back-bencher's lot significantly changed. One might make impressive speeches, but the armour was not for penetration. Government did what it had always intended to do. It is not Parliament which is sovereign; it is the Executive. A debate may shift it a little this way or that; but, broadly speaking, what the Administration wills will be. There is perhaps one qualification which one ought to make: one could make one's own side think, and this might, at a later juncture, affect the Government, either helping it or hindering it. On one occasion, following in the debate the late Hugh Gaitskell, I supported the initial attempt to enter the European Community.

Gaitskell was not at that stage (6 June 1962) opposed to entry into the EEC, but insisted that conditions be met which safeguarded the Commonwealth. He feared for the Commonwealth on three counts. First the preferences which had previously been given to Commonwealth manufactured products would, on United Kingdom entry into the EEC, be given instead to manufactured products from the EEC. Secondly, the protection envisaged by the EEC for agriculture, a much greater protection than given by the United Kingdom, would disrupt the Commonwealth. Thirdly, and most importantly, the political institutions of the EEC – an independent commission and decisions by a majority vote in a council of Ministers – might imply indifference to the rest of the world, might lead to a third force wanting its own nuclear weapons and breaking away from the Atlantic Alliance. Under such institutions he doubted whether the Commonwealth would survive.[7]

I replied that there was a better chance of obtaining the conditions we wanted if our attitude to the Community was judged by the latter to be sympathetic [contrast with Mrs Thatcher's attitude]. 'Each one of us taking part in the debate is an ambassador for his country.' '. . . we should speak, not to those in Europe who do not want us in, but to those who do want us in, and it was in this respect, it seemed to me, that the speech of the Right Honourable Gentleman [Gaitskell] fell short'. The Community, I went on to say, was a novel concept, both economically and politically. It was more than a free-trade area, in that it attempted to meet in common the problems resulting from internal free trade – unemployment in a given area, balance of payments difficulties for this country or that, an attempt by one country to

[7]   Official Reports, Parliamentary Debates, Vo. 661, cols. 507–27.

export to others its depression. This was way beyond Britain's earlier concept of a European free-trade area, which should now give way to a superior idea. Politically the Community differed from other international organisations all of which had been governed by the rule of unanimity. As a result their capacity for action was extremely limited, and it was no surprise that all the glistening proposals for international economic and political collaboration which were born on the morrow of the war now lay dust-laden on the shelves. The key characteristic of the Community's constitution was the independent origin of proposals made. This was more important than the other characteristic of majority rule, for it was the independent origin of proposals which made them acceptable. The Commonwealth was not an organisation of this kind. But

> We cannot, just because we are leaders of a loose organisation, say that on that account we should not enter a tighter organisation. That would be tantamount to saying that we in this country cannot enter any more progressive international organisation than a mere co-operative association of independent sovereign states. I cannot think that would be writing a creditable page in the history of Commonwealth.

I concluded by suggesting that a relationship should be established between the Community and the Commonwealth. In temperate foodstuffs the Commonwealth countries subsidised competition against one another, with the result of mutually ruinous surpluses. There would be a better chance of action if a proposal came from an independent organisation. Similarly the European technique could be used to deal with the poorer countries.

> the basic problems of the Commonwealth transcend Commonwealth. They are world problems and in facing them we are driven to fuse the Commonwealth into a larger structure and a wider framework... we should not try to protect the Commonwealth concept as we have known it... There is still enough political genius left in this country to give the new ideas in Europe a wider significance, a signficance which otherwise ... they would far less easily acquire.[8]

I was told that the speech exercised considerable influence on my back-bench colleagues, who were riven over the entire issue of entry into the Community. Whether that is true or not I do not know. If true,

---

[8] Ibid., cols. 527–37.

then influence over the thoughts of one's own side represents the potential summit of a back-bencher's achievement, for I cannot contend to have affected subsequently the attitudes of governments.

While I supported the Government in its attempt to enter the European Economic Community, I considered that the negotiations were unimaginatively conducted. The same is probably true of all the subsequent negotiations – as a country we have never understood what the Community was all about. Friends of mine on the French negotiating team told me that it was never their intention to talk of pineapples and bananas; yet that is the level down to which we dragged them. The French team's advice to General de Gaulle was that the negotiations were running into the sands and that all he had to do was to sit back and wait. Why then did he, in January 1963, declare a veto? Was it his love of the dramatic gesture? Or was there truth in the story that on a Saturday morning before Christmas the French Ambassador met Mr Edward Heath, the main British negotiator, shopping in Harrods? 'How are the negotiations going?' asked the French Ambassador. 'Fine', Mr Heath is reported to have replied. On that same Saturday evening I entertained Sir Eric (now Lord) Roll, Mr Heath's chief adviser, to dinner. I put to him the same question as the French Ambassador is related to have put to Mr Heath. 'Fine', was the answer. There was no reason why Lord Roll should seek to deceive me. I suspect he had no idea that he was facing failure.

If my speech in the House of Commons was a summit I also descended at the same time to the nadir. My constituency, a leafy suburb of Birmingham, contained no immigrants. But the inner circle of the city teemed with them. Anyone travelling to the centre of the city had to traverse that compound of decayed private landlordism and an England that still beckoned to immigrants. My Conservative colleagues in Birmingham raised their voices increasingly against the incoming tide. Their cries made me unhappy and gradually I began to speak out against them. Morally I accepted immigrants as fellow members of the human kind; the world was increasingly becoming multi-racial; were we, as the leader of the Commonwealth, to exempt ourselves from the duty imposed on us by this movement? Economically we were growing slowly in relation to other countries and lacked the domestic reserves of labour which might help to accelerate our momentum. 'It is interesting to speculate on how the trend in output might have been affected if government had not chosen, for social reasons, to impose restrictions on immigration in the early 1960s, thus preventing the domestic labour force from being augmented by immigrants to the extent that it was in West Germany and France.'[9]

The government restrictions referred to were those contained in the first bill against immigration launched by Butler in 1962. I had returned the previous evening from the United States and was not prepared enough to take part in the debate. But I listened to Butler's opening speech. The one piece of legislation on British nationality at that time was the British Nationality Act of 1948. It distinguished between two types: citizens of the then called Dominions, independent of Britain; and citizens of the United Kingdom and the colonies. The holder of a British passport was thus a citizen of the United Kingdom and the colonies. By the same token a citizen of the colonies was a citizen of the United Kingdom. There was a rationale in this in that some of the Caribbean islands had been uninhabited when first explored by the British; it was the British who plucked planters from other places and settled them on the islands. English was the only language they knew. They were therefore creations of the British with a moral as well as a legal title to be called British.

Butler's bill to limit immigrations, without changing the British Nationality Act of 1948, chose to ignore its implications. Henceforth those allowed to enter the United Kingdom had either to be born here or were to hold passports issued by the United Kingdom Government. A Carribean therefore, while British under the British Nationality Act of 1948, but who had his passport issued by a Caribbean authority, could no longer enter; while still British, he was debarred from entry into Britain. This piece of chicanery was wrapped in a load of rhetoric – such as the British Commonwealth's representing 'one quarter of the population of the globe' ... with the prospect of 'virtually limitless immigration'.[10] In fact the figures appeared to show that immigration waxed as the economy boomed, and waned when the economy weakened.

I was appalled and did not vote. Mrs Thatcher, on the other hand, voted for.

The climax was reached in 1964, when the Conservative leadership in Birmingham decided to make immigration the main election issue. The decision followed the taking of an opinion survey, which indicated

[9] Matthews, Feinstein, and Odling-Smee, *British Economic Growth 1856–1973*, Stamford University Press, 1982, p. 513.
[10] Official Report, Parliamentary Debates, Vol. 649, cols. 687, ff.

'colour' to be predominant in people's minds. Mr (now Lord) Geoffrey-Lloyd, distant heir to Joseph Chamberlain as leader of the Birmingham Conservative 'caucus', convened a lunch of Birmingham Conservative members and candidates to discuss the outcome. Neither Edward (later Lord) Boyle nor I was able to be present. We read, however, of the decision in the newspapers. Later I was approached by Geoffrey Lloyd in the lobbies of the House of Commons. He said that my colleagues were apprehensive lest I should make difficulties for them. I replied that I would not set out to make difficulties, but if asked questions at the impending election would reply as I thought appropriate. I then set seriously to study the question. Early in the new Parliament that followed I made known my contrary views. Every word I subsequently uttered was closely scrutinised to see whether or not it was in accord with 'Birmingham'. Official Conservatism in Birmingham had identified itself with racism, and thus began my alienation from the Conservative Party.

Shortly afterwards an attempt was made to oust me. Among the 'ousters' was the Association chairman, who until then had been friendly towards me. At the relevant meeting, I won handsomely. After the meeting there was a press conference. My chairman was asked what role 'colour' had played in the entire affair. He answered, 'None'. 'Colour', he said, was irrelevant to Hall Green. I rejoined that no citizen of Birmingham, however directly untouched by 'colour', could be indifferent to the plight of the inner city. Not long after my chairman was made Lord Mayor of the City of Birmingham.

3
THE MARKET

Five years after my entry into the House of Commons, I was made, in 1955, Minister of Fuel and Power. I have never been a parliamentary or Junior Minister, and such as I have seen have played no great part in the determination of policy. There were those in the press who ascribed my abrupt advancement to a single speech which I had made on the coal industry. I question whether this could have been the whole truth. The scribes had forgotten that Anthony Eden, the Prime Minister, had associations with Durham, a mining area, had therefore an interest in mining, and that one of his first acts as Prime Minister was to go down a pit. Nor were they to know that in the early years after the Second World War I was associated with Eden in trying to promote the concept of a 'property-owing democracy'. I moved a resolution to this effect at an early post-war Conservative Party conference; I was to have been supported by Lord Salisbury (Cranborne, I believe, he then was), but at the last moment he could not make it.

From time to time the Conservative Party, conscious of its modern identification with capitalism, has made the odd attempt to overcome the divisions between capital and labour. Disraeli did so through the creation of Young England, a movement led by a few aristocrats. Eden did so through the idea of a 'property-owning democracy'.

Each time the attempt has failed. The failure could have been due to the exigencies of the moment – for example, Eden's preoccupation with foreign affairs. It could also be due to deeper causes – the inability of the Conservative Party to loosen its ties with capital. It is the latter explanation, I suspect, which is the real truth. As a result, the trumpeted phrase 'One Nation' conceals a permanent vacuum in policy.

Be that as it may, I found myself Minister of Fuel and Power. To the popular mind the Ministry had vaguely to do with three allegedly inefficient nationalised industries – coal, electricity, and gas – and one privately owned, and therefore inevitably efficient industry – oil. In

19

the 1970s, when the idea of the giant Department became fashionable, the Ministry became part of the Department of Trade and Industry, though heaven alone knows why. Later heaven was defied and the Ministry reverted to its original compact form, though under a grander name – the Department of Energy.

What then are the functions of the Department of Energy? The latest exposition known to me is by Mr Nigel Lawson, when, as the head of the Department, he spoke to the International Association of Energy Economists on 28 June 1982. He spoke thus: 'I do not see the Government's task as being to try and plan the future shape of energy production and consumption . . . Our task is rather to set a framework which will ensure that the market operates in the energy sector with a minimum of distortion and that energy is produced and consumed efficiently.'[1] This statement was repeated early in 1984 by a deputy secretary of the Department speaking to the Cambridge Energy Research Unit.

The statement quoted ignores the responsibilities of the Ministry of Fuel and Power as laid down in the Ministry of Fuel and Power Act of 1945. That act placed on the Minister a general duty of 'securing the effective and *co-ordinated* [my italics] development of coal, petroleum and other sources of fuel and power . . .'. The case for co-ordination lies in the fact that one fuel can be substituted for another – coal or fuel oil, for example, can be used for the generation of electrical power; a gap between the supply available of one and the demand for it can be made good by another – a shortage in the supply of gas can be filled either by imports of gas or by electricity; different fuels have different effects on the environment and the security of supply can similarly vary from fuel to fuel. Each source of fuel therefore has implications for the others. And all of them, with the exception of water, which is scarcely used in this country, represent deposits in the ground which are subject to depletion. Even uranium, the basis of nuclear power, as now known, is exhaustible, though alternatives, such as thorium, can be found. The trouble was that, while the Minister had a formal duty to co-ordinate, he did not have the power, each industry being run by a separate board with its own statutory responsibilities. The exercise of those separate responsibilities does not necessarily lead to the operation of a market with the minimum of 'distortion', whatever that ambiguous word might mean.

[1]   *Energy Paper Number 51*, HMSO, London, 1982, p. 3.

Nor does the statement recognise the attempts made to remedy after the event the defects of the 1945 act. The most important of these was the so-called Ridley Report,[2] published in 1952, which describes nationalisation as having made higher the 'walls of severance'. At that time the supplies of oil were limited, the great Saudi Arabian lake not having then been discovered. The main preoccupation therefore was with coal. Broadly speaking, the Ridley Committee wanted to see competition between the fuel and power industries according to their prices. But what prices? Short-term, long-term? And if long-term, were they to be prices related to the costs of future additions to supply or to the average of costs incurred in the past? On this last issue the committee was divided clean down the middle.

Faced with its own internal divisions and a statute which precluded the interposition of an executive body between the several industries and the Minister, the committee took circumventing action. It recommended the establishment of a Tariffs Advisory Committee which would report on cases where there appeared to be a conflict between the pricing policy of a particular Board and the wider national interest; the appointment of a Joint Fuel and Power Board which would concern itself with new techniques and with research and development affecting more than one industry; and the formation by the Ministry, in co-operation with local authorities, of a service which should provide a fuel information service in large towns. To the best of my knowledge none of the Ridley recommendations was acted on. The committee, nonetheless, had a point; electricity tariffs were deliberately kept low to encourage consumption, with the result of an undue demand on the country's capital resources. Hugh Gaitskell, while Minister, railed in vain against this. In addition investment in coal lagged way behind investment in electricity. The lack of co-ordination was leading to an unbalanced energy programme. As Minister, I did my best to secure from officials a statement on energy policy. I got nowhere. The same was true of all my successors. Not one of them has ever had an energy policy, except in so far as one has arisen indirectly through the approval or non-approval of investment projects.

The passive statement quoted from Mr Nigel Lawson contrasts starkly with the situation in France. There the Government, so far from sitting back, acts positively with regard to investment in energy through the Agence Française pour la Maîtrise de l'Energie. The

---

[2] Report of the Committee on National Policy for the Use of Fuel and Power Resources, Cmd. 8647.

broad purposes of the Agence are two: to reduce the rate at which energy is consumed by an expanding economy and to substitute domestic forms of energy for those now imported. The methods used to attain these purposes are research and development, undertaken by the Agence itself or in conjunction with industry, and the dissemination of information about energy management by changing the projected investment decisions of firms and by giving them financial help. In the case of firms of size an approved investment in energy might qualify for a subsidy of 20 per cent of the cost, while in the case of a public organisation such as a school or hospital the subsidy could be as much as 30 per cent or more. Small and medium-sized firms are in addition given the help of professional experts. The quantitative target set for all these activities is a reduction of 20–25 per cent in imports of energy by 1990. All this is, with a vengeance, an attempt to 'plan the future shape of energy production and consumption'.

Finally, the Minister's professed attachment to the operation of the market ignores the fact that today's markets are to a large extent determined by past events – errors of judgement, mistaken investment decisions, miscalculations of demand. The prices of the present are to a large extent the debris left by the past. They do not do what prices should do – offer a guide to action for the future. To act in accordance with today's market manifestations is to act upon the impact of present demand on the supplies arising from earlier mistakes. The result could well be to perpetuate past errors. To have continued to consume, for example, electricity rather than gas because its price was kept cheap would have been to ignore the future source of gas in the North Sea and the increase in the price of oil as a source of electrical power. It would therefore delay the future evolution of energy policy altogether.

Even if the slate could be wiped clean and the market restarted afresh, its signals might be valid for today and tomorrow, but they would not necessarily be relevant to an act of investment which has to stretch over the next 25 years or, in the case of a pit, possibly 80 years.

Investments of importance in energy are all of this long-term nature and risky; they therefore require for their execution a judgement, based on the extreme uncertainty of the future in general and of individual sources of energy in particular. They cannot be based on any precise prediction and cannot possibly therefore produce a market framework in which 'energy is produced and consumed efficiently'.

The Minister had enunciated, in relation to energy, a primitive theory according to which supply and demand in a simple market can be quickly adjusted. In a domain like energy the theory was irrelevant. It is not market forces which determine economic events or the fate of nations; it is, more than anything else, technology, which may be started decades before its market manifestation. This conclusion will emerge more strikingly when each fuel and power industry is examined in turn.

4

COAL

Events obliged me to try to tackle first the problem of coal. The new Chancellor with whom I had to deal was Mr Harold Macmillan. He was ostensibly more of a Keynesian than his predecessor, Butler. In the hearing of Lord Roberthall[1] he said: 'I hate capitalism', meaning that he hated the unemployment resulting from the fluctuations which may be inherent in capitalism. The label 'Keynesian' attached to Mr Macmillan by Lord Roberthall may be said later to have been borne out by Mr Macmillan's fumbling approaches to an 'incomes policy', though according to the late Lord Boyle he was opposed to the introduction by his Chancellor, Selwyn Lloyd, of a formal policy.[2]

Mr Macmillan, the Keynesian, had inherited from his predecessor, Butler, a boom, with the usual threatened run on sterling. Butler's budget in the autumn of 1955 had been ineffective to stem it. The language which his successor, Mr Macmillan, used in an attempt to abate the boom was identical with that used today by a monetarist Sir Geoffrey Howe or a monetarist Mr Lawson. As a nation we had taken on more than we could afford; we were placing an undue strain on our resources; since the war we had had continuous inflation, though it can scarcely have exceeded 3 per cent a year; in particular expenditure on defence and on military research and development was on the up and up. Over 30 years, straddling changes in economic fashion, the language has not changed. Perhaps the problem has not changed. Perhaps there is just one permanent problem to the solution of which there are slight differences of approach, theologically magnified.

Be that as it may, the order of the day, as now, was 'cuts, cuts, cuts'. Not cuts with an emphasis here rather than there, not cuts with a strategic purpose, just cuts in all areas of public investment. With

---

[1] Lord Roberthall, British Oral Archives of Political and Administrative History, British Library of Political and Economic Science.
[2] Lord Boyle, British Oral Archives of Political and Administrative History, British Library of Political and Economic Science.

others I was one of the victims. A Martian might have asked: 'Why not cut private investment, representing roughly half of all investment?' He would have been told that, with the abolition in 1954 of all controls over building, there was no direct method of affecting private investment, only the indirect methods of higher interest rates and a lessened demand by the Government. The re-introduction of building controls was, however, being considered and the Cabinet agreed to limit imports if the economic situation continued to deteriorate. Meanwhile, public investment had to bear the brunt. Some small attempt, however, was made to cut consumption. A reduction in food subsidies was proposed. The late Iain Macleod, then Minister of Labour, protested, fearing an adverse effect on wages. But he was over-ridden.

Relatively, one of the biggest cuts in capital investment was asked of coal – the cancellation of the whole of the projected additional investment of £7 million in 1956 over the £100 million estimated to have been spent in 1955. I protested, and sought a deal. I agreed to defer the construction of new power stations and to cut the gas investment programme by more than was asked for, provided that the planned reduction in coal investment was limited to £5 million. The deal was accepted.

Why did I fight so fiercely for coal? The reasons are perhaps clearer to me now than they were at the time. All the fuel and power industries that were nationalised were highly fragmented. In the case of coal, of the 1,400 pits nationalised 480 were small mines in the hands of individual owners. As the Reid Report put it: 'In Britain, the fact that ownership of the mineral has been in private hands has often resulted in unduly small or awkwardly shaped leaseholders; in the development of an excessive number of mines of insufficient capacity for the best mining practice; and in inadequate attention to the conservation of the national resource.'[3] The coal industry may have been nationalised to secure a 'commanding height of the economy', though commanding heights change. But there was a strong pragmatic case for nationalisation – the fragmented nature of the industry militated against investment and against research and development.

The plight of the industry on the eve of nationalisation as described in the Reid Report was echoed by Lord Fleck, chairman of a committee nominally set up by the National Coal Board itself but probably owing its inspiration to the part-time members of the Board acting

[3] Technical Advisory Committee on Coal Mining, 1945, Cmd. 6610, p. 128.

with the connivance of the Ministry. The Fleck Report recorded: 'From the end of the First World War to the end of the Second, the industry was starved of capital and of technical men. At nationalisation, it was, for the most part, backward both in general and in technical management. The condition of many of the collieries was poor.'[4] Illustrative of this was the fact that, while I was Minister, three-quarters of the coal produced came from pits sunk before 1918. In addition, post-war investment in coal had lagged behind that in customer industries, particularly electricity and steel. The nationalisation of the coal industry made possible a degree of investment far greater than that previously undertaken. It did not of itself, however, answer the crucial question: at what output should the investment aim? The answer given more than once presaged the dispute over pit closures which ultimately broke out in 1984.

From the outset the National Coal Board was divided on the issue of the output to be aimed for. On the one hand, there were those, including some engineers and financial controllers, who wanted a small but 'viable' industry, concentrated in the geologically better areas. They could be said to be the predecessors of Mr Ian MacGregor, appointed chairman of the NCB in 1983.

The difficulty is that they never clearly defined the concept of 'viability'. Presumably they meant, as Mr MacGregor appears to have meant, that costs should not exceed the price obtainable in the market. What matters, however, as a guide to investment, which may not yield coal for several decades, is not the present market price, but the future price. Unhappily the future is shrouded in darkness. Two scenarios are possible. The oil reserves of the world are smaller than the coal reserves; with the exhaustion of the oil reserves, the long-term real price of oil will rise, with coal also rising in price in sympathy. This scenario would imply a larger output than that sought by those concerned with making the industry 'viable' in the narrowest sense.

Alternatively there is much coal in the world – in the United States, South Africa, and in the Communist block, the latter being the largest, though not necessarily a dominant producer. The real price of coal could therefore remain stable for a long time to come. This scenario gives the benefit of the doubt to the protagonists of a small and 'viable' industry.

Opposed to them were those generally, though not exclusively, on

---

[4]   Report of the Advisory Committee on Organisation, 1955, p. 8.

the marketing side, who, seeing on the morrow of the Second World War a world shortage of coal, wanted the maximum possible expansion; blind to the future advent of oil and gas, they believed that the price could be pushed high enough to render an expanded industry profitable. In addition, they disliked the diversion of coal traffic entailed by the concentration of production in the geologically most favourable areas. They were aided and abetted by the critics of nationalisation, who complained that the Coal Board was not producing enough. The National Plan for Coal, completed in 1950, was, as a result a fudge – setting a target of 230–250 million tons a year for the period 1961–5, as compared with the then output of just over 200 million tons a year and the previous peak of nearly 290 million tons achieved in 1913, from which date the decline of the industry began.

The over-ambitious nature of the National Plan quickly became apparent, although it is fair to add that a degree of frustration arose from the imposed curtailment of expenditure due to the rearmament occasioned by the Korean war. The greater frustration, however, arose from over-optimism in the first place. Even without this excess of optimism all forecasts of demand for coal would have gone astray with the advent of natural gas. The initial plan had been estimated to cost in total something less than £650 million, an estimated annual rate of expenditure of around £40 million, some two-thirds to come from depreciation provisions. This figure represented a serious underestimate of the cost of renovating old mines and sinking new ones. Inevitably, the plan fell behind schedule. For example, of £128 million supposed to have been spent since 1947, schemes amounting to only £11 million had been completed by the end of 1955. The result was that, if the earlier target in output was to be attained, a higher capital expenditure than that earlier contemplated was needed. This history was continuously repeated.

I was the recipient, only a few years after the publication of the National Plan for Coal, of a revised plan, officially known as Investing in Coal. The new plan aimed at the old target – roughly, 240 million tons by 1965, at a now larger total cost of £1,000 million over ten years. Unaware as I then was of the internal warfare taking place within the Coal Board over the level of future output, as was also, I believe, the Ministry, I reduced the output target to under 230 million tons. My mistake, in retrospect, was not to reduce enough. I also stipulated that, of the total financial requirement of £1,000 million, £350 million should be borrowed from the Treasury, the rest being found from the Board's own resources, which was possible only by raising prices. This I did to meet the Treasury's insistence on keeping down the Government's spending on investment, but, as will be seen later, the Treasury was torn on the issue whether investment should be financed by borrowing or by raising prices. Finally, I laid it down that the Board's annual capital expenditure should be subject to supervision by the Government, thereby acting possibly unconstitutionally, there being no provision in the Coal Industry Act for annual reviews of capital expenditure. All that the act provided for was agreement on the general lines of an investment programme which might last several years.

In spite of these modifications, I believed it right to continue investment in coal. My reasons were three. First, even to produce an output lower than that fixed in the National Plan extra investment was needed. Secondly, trouble was already looming in the Middle East, trouble that was later to vent itself in the nationalisation of the Suez Canal and the war that followed. I played no part in the management of the British side of that ill-fated war, this having been remitted to a Cabinet sub-committee known as the Egypt Committee. Thirdly, our lagging coal production was alienating European friends. In particular, France, which had previously relied to a large extent on British coal exports, was forced to import from Germany. In 1938 the United Kingdom exported to France over 6 million tonnes of coal; in 1951 the export can scarcely have been more than 500,000 tonnes. The cessation of exports to France was certainly not in accord with the spirit of the recently established Council of Association between the United Kingdom and the European Coal and Steel Community.

The Council of Association had been formed because of Britain's refusal to join the Community itself. The late M. Jean Monnet, President of the Community, had come to London to try to persuade Britain to enter. He had met Sir Stafford Cripps and Sir Edwin (now Lord) Plowden, and was given a blank refusal. The Council of Association was designed to fill the gap. I cannot recall that it accomplished anything of significance, but it gave me the opportunity of becoming friendly with Jean Monnet. We used to pace up and down his garden, wondering what he should do. Was he to continue as President of the Community or was he to adopt a freelance position in Paris and campaign for a wider Community: rightly in retrospect he decided on the latter course. It was thus that I learned of the novel nature of what was later to be the European Economic Community and was captivated by it. Long after I had ceased to be Minister of Fuel and Power I used regularly to visit him. On one of these occasions he was staying at Brown's Hotel, in London, on the second floor. He decided to take me to the ground floor. We entered the lift. He pressed the ground-floor button. Nothing happened. He pressed again. Nothing. As we descended on foot, he said: 'I told you; Britain *will* enter the Community.'

But to return to coal investment, notwithstanding my doubts about 'Investing in Coal' I ran into trouble with Conservative backbenchers. They complained that there had been no technical assessment of the programme. This was true, the Ministry lacking technical expertise in all the industries sponsored by it, a lack which has continued to the present day. To have examined the programme technically would in fact have been in contravention of the act, which limited the Minister's functions to approving the 'lines' on which the Board acted in framing its programmes. The doctrine had been firmly laid down by that strong-minded character, Sir Donald Fergusson, private secretary to Winston Churchill when the latter was Chancellor of the Exchequer between 1924 and 1929, and the first Permanent Secretary of the post-war Ministry of Fuel and Power: 'Any control exercised by Government . . . should be control over global figures based on general principles and . . . not . . . by detailed analysis and criticism of individual schemes.'

From the high plateau there was a rapid descent down the slope. Under pressure at a later date from the House of Commons Select Committee on Nationalised Industries the Board agreed to give, in relation to each major project, the estimated financial yield, the estimated output and productivity, the types of coal to be worked and the estimated year of completion. Had I still been Minister, I doubt whether I would have pushed the Board to this concession. But pushed it was, and mistakenly it yielded. For suppose none of these estimates was achieved. What then? There was no control which the Ministry had over individual pits. Nor had the Ministry any power of dismissal, and if things went wrong it was far from clear who was responsible. All the Ministry had was a power to refuse monies. And to refuse monies would have been to cut off one's nose to spite one's face.

The back-benchers' more fundamental complaint, however, was that the Coal Board was intending to borrow, even the limited amount suggested, backed by a Treasury guarantee. Were the Treasury ever called upon to act in accordance with its guarantee, it could do so only with money drawn from the tax payer. In theory, if not in practice, the House of Commons is the taxpayer's guardian. Should it not therefore discharge its required role by scrutinising, even in greater detail than the Ministry had done, the Coal Board's programme?

The complaint, inspired by whatever motives, drew attention to a real anomaly. The late Herbert Morrison, in framing the acts of nationalisation, considered that the nationalised industries would operate more efficiently if kept at a certain distance from Government, and not treated as a Government Department. The House of Commons, on the other hand, has over time claimed a greater and greater degree of control, the fact of the Treasury guarantee giving a plausible justification to the claim. There is no possible reconciliation between these different points of view, though some kind of bridge can be erected between them through the efficiency audit begun by the National Board for Prices and Incomes and now continued by the Monopolies and Mergers Commission. Though the Morrisonian concept of an 'arm's length' relationship between a nationalised industry and a Government Department has been eroded at the edges, it remains in my view fundamentally sound and, for my part, I would continue to live with the anomaly. The only thing to be said for 'privatisation' is that, where accomplished, it would solve the insoluble.

My contretemps with the Conservative back-benchers led me to the belief that a Conservative Government is incapable of running a mixed economy. It does not believe in one. It believes only in a private economy, something impossible to return to, as its own attitude towards agriculture shows. Nor have I been alone in this belief. It was shared by, among others, the late Sir Harold Hartley, chairman of a Commission of Energy set up by the then Organisation for European Economic Co-operation (OEEC). While advocating heavy investment in coal, he wrote: 'It is not statesmanship to go on conducting a vendetta against nationalisation. Nationalised industries must be led and inspired.'[5]

I myself expressed a similar thought in the speech in which I pushed the investment programme through Parliament. 'The lack of understanding', I said, 'was aggravated by the attitude which said, on the one hand, 'There is nothing wrong with nationalisation' and with

---

[5]   Forward, 9.6.1956, Sir Harold Hartley, Papers, Archives Centre, Churchill College, Cambridge.

the extremism, on the other hand, which said, 'There is nothing right with nationalisation . . . If this industry needs anything at all, it is surely objective understanding.'[6]

It is time, however, to return to the case of the internal war. Long after I had left the Ministry of Fuel and Power the war between, on the one hand, some engineers and financial controllers, and, on the other, the marketeers, aided and abetted by the Conservative opposition, continued. There was a short intermission during the chairmanship of Sir James Bowman, a chairmanship which was unexpected. The Fleck Report had been so critical of the Board's performance that it was expected that Sir Hubert Houldsworth, the then chairman, would resign. He did not; he clung on, his action leading in protest to the departure from the Board of two part-time members, Sir Geoffrey (later Lord) Heyworth, who had in 1951 objected to Sir Hubert's appointment, an objection repeated in 1955, and Mr Jack Hambro. Sir Hubert was therefore my inheritance. I doubt whether constitutionally I could have forced him to resign. But providence intervened; he died. I appointed Sir James Bowman as his successor, with Mr (later Sir) Joseph Latham as his deputy. Under their regime those wanting a small viable industry began to have their way.

Their opponents, however, were soon on the warpath again. They found a champion in Lord Robens, who hoisted a target of 200 million tons of coal a year, allegedly to boost morale. Lord Robens is credited with having conducted a stealthy closure of pits. How closures on an adequate scale can be reconciled with so high a target is not easy to understand. Sir Derek (later Lord) Ezra followed in his footsteps, announcing in 1974 a third investment programme, totalling £1,400 million in the ten-year period up to 1985. This third programme envisaged 42 million tonnes of new capacity by 1985; so far only some 30 million tonnes appear to be available. Had a policy of closures been steadily followed, the National Coal Board would not have faced large arrears of closures in 1984.

There is a great deal of confusion over the question of closures. 'A pit is exhausted when the cost of getting the remaining coal becomes too great in relation to the price obtainable. Exhaustion is therefore an economic rather than a technical concept.'[7] It is the difference between an economic and a technical concept which is at the heart of the

6   Parliamentary Debates, House of Commons, Vo. 552, cols. 1439, 1440.
7   P. Lesley Cook and A. J. Surrey, *Energy Policy*, Martin Robertson, London, 1977, p. 81.

dispute between the National Coal Board and the National Union of Mineworkers, although I myself would be inclined to interpret the economic concept of closure in the light more of the future than the present price. As I have said, it is possible that the real price of coal will remain stable for a long time to come, in which case the benefit of the doubt has to be given to those favouring a smaller rather than a large industry.

While capital was thus being continuously injected into the industry output declined between 1950 and 1975, after which it roughly stabilised. In sum, the drag of uneconomic pits was stemming the benefits expected from new and reconstructed pits. Nemesis came with the recession of 1980, demand falling and the stock of unsaleable coal piling high, bringing in train high interest charges. The collapse of the market aggravated the problems of an over-expanded industry and precipitated the dispute over closures.

Nor was this the only cost which the expansionist inflicted on the industry. The Central Electricity Board, dependent on coal for some 80 per cent of its fuel, was effectively tied up as a market, agreeing in 1979 to take up until 1985 an annual amount of 75 million tonnes (later reduced) provided that prices did not rise faster than the rate of inflation, and keeping cheaper imports to a minimum.

In addition large sums of public money were poured into the industry to cover losses and to help meet the costs of reducing capacity. Grant aid from the Government amounted in 1981–2 to no less than £575 million.[8]

Finally, in 1962 an excise duty was imposed on imported fuel oil. Cunningly suggested to the Chancellor by Lord Robens on the eve of the budget, it was represented as a means of raising revenue. In reality it was a measure to protect coal, though it was a measure of diminishing value, the worth of the duty, which was expressed in absolute terms, falling as inflation accelerated.

What we do not know is, had imports been more freely allowed, how much cheaper the cost of energy to British industry would have been and how many more workers would have retained their jobs while more miners lost theirs. The Monopolies and Mergers Commission in its report on the coal industry does not attempt this calculation. In the last analysis delay in the closure of uneconomic pits has been at the expense of other parts of British industry, and while British miners

[8]   The Monopolies and Mergers Commission, Report on Coal Industry, Cmnd. 8920, p. 363.

might have been kept in employment, British workers in other industries might have been made unemployed because of the price of British coal.

We have then in coal a highly subsidised and protected industry. It is true that the subsidy is less than that given to coal in other countries. Nonetheless it has added to the undue inflation of the industry. The picture simply does not fit into Mr Lawson's 'Framework which will ensure that the market operates . . . and that energy is produced . . . efficiently'. It does not square with any concept, least of all a theoretical concept, of the market.

I had injected into the coal industry a modicum of investment, though without awareness of the full ambition of the plans to follow; I had also in part re-modelled the Board, though not to my full satisfaction – I sought for eight whole months outside the industry for a successor to Joseph Latham as a finance director, but then had to turn inside; in addition I wanted to appoint as personnel director somebody outside the industry; my man was named but my successor ducked the issue. The National Union of Mineworkers (NUM) wanted their own nominee, Mr Arthur Horner, who happened to be a Communist. I had no objection to him as a person – I liked him and he was kind to me. Meeting me in the train one day after my departure from the Ministry, he asked: 'Why did they remove you? It cannot have been on grounds of incompetence.' My objection was not to Arthur Horner, who came from my home town, but rather to the concept with which the NUM invested their nominee. In their eyes he was there to represent the NUM view. I, on the other hand, felt that his duty was to represent the interests of the Board as a whole. I thought I had done my best by the industry. However, there were further problems to follow.

The Coal Board had, in the spring of 1956, conceded a wage increase of 9 per cent. As far as I remember, there was no consultation with me, nor did the statute require any. The rate of increase in output per man was nothing like this figure, and so I proposed – possibly improperly – a price increase of 8 per cent, though whether the Cabinet immediately agreed to this I cannot recollect. I was anxious only to ensure that the price increase should follow quickly on the wage increase, in order to demonstrate the link between the two. 'The horse', I wrote, 'is out of the stable, and the farther we allow it to roam the more difficult it will be to catch up with it.'

The proposed price increase was soon ensnared in an initiative of Mr Macmillan's as Chancellor. He had observed that wages had been outstripping prices and considered therefore that the Government should call upon both sides of industry for stability in wages and prices. He was to see in the first instance the TUC. My immediate concern was the proposed price increase in coal. Was the Coal Board to go ahead or was I, assuming I had the power, a doubtful assumption, to instruct it to stabilise?

I had already agreed to a reduction in the coal industry's borrowing for investment, expecting the Board to find part of the required amount from an increase in price. Which did the Chancellor now want – a higher borrowing with a stabilised price, or the lower borrowing agreed upon with a price increase? The Chancellor was reflecting the Treasury schizophrenia earlier referred to: was investment to be financed by borrowing or by higher prices? He equivocated; he just did not know. In these circumstances the price increase went ahead.

The Central Electricity Authority, under Lord Citrine, decided, without consultation with me, to hold electricity tariffs at their then level, leaving the increase in the price of coal out of account. Lord Citrine was giving his own interpretation of 'the national interest'. I accepted the situation, holding that I had no statutory power to object. But no incident could have illustrated more vividly the Ridley Committee's point that the charges of the fuel and power industries should be placed on some more rational basis than the whims of competing Boards. As for the increase in the price of coal, the Coal Board as a result made a profit, while fares on the railways were frozen, and the railways, to the best of my knowledge, have ever since remained in deficit.

Mr Macmillan's ambivalence was a real one. Which in fact was the more inflationary? An increase in borrowing from the Exchequer or an increase in the price of an important material, rippling its way through other prices? The ambivalence remained, to be encountered again later in life when I became Chairman of the National Board for Prices and Incomes. I know of no academic study of this dilemma and to this day I remain myself in a state of ignorance.

5
ELECTRICITY

The next industry with which I had to deal was electricity. The National Coal Board had ostensibly set up its own committee to enquire into itself. In the case of electricity my predecessor had set up an outside committee of enquiry, chaired by Sir Edwin Herbert (later Lord Tangley). It was I, not my predecessor, who inherited the so-called Herbert Report. It was the first report that I had seen on an aspect of government by a committee composed principally, though not exclusively, of industrialists. I have seen others since. The more I have seen, the lower my opinion of industrialists and their reports has sunk, for industrialists dip into the alien world of politics and know not what they do.

Like coal, electricity was a fragmented industry. Its origins go back to, roughly, 1882. The laying of electrical cables necessitated the break-up of pavements, the responsibility of municipal undertakings. Accordingly an act of 1882 gave municipal undertakings the right to manufacture electricity or give others a licence to manufacture. As the uses of electricity expanded, from lighting to heating and power, and as the technology advanced, the administrative unit, whether municipal or private, fell out of date. Somehow or other it had to be expanded to correspond with the expanding industry. Administrative expansion entailed an assimilation of frequencies – there were often different voltages on opposite sides of the same street – and a readiness to connect generating and distributing stations of different degrees of power. The administrative units, however, would not voluntarily come together. The ferocity of the debate between the champions of municipal undertakings (one was Joseph Chamberlain) and the upholders of private enterprise was every bit as intense as that between nationalisers and anti-nationalisers after 1945.

The organisation of the industry was in marked contrast with that of Sweden, where undertakings could be owned in part by municipalities, in part by private individuals, working in full collaboration with the state. In the event of a dispute between any of the three parties it was remitted to arbitration.[1] There can be little doubt that the British organisation held up the progress of the industry.

' "In the age of steam', a factory inspector was already noting sadly in 1901, 'this country led the way, whereas in the age of electricity, we seem to follow America and other countries." '[2] It is odd that citizens of this country spent the early decades of this century electrifying railways all over the world, while the development of electricity at home was neglected. Some 25 years after the start of the century it was no different, Sir Philip Cunliffe-Lister (later Lord Swinton), Baldwin's President of the Board of Trade, saying: 'electricity . . . is so inefficient today in this country that it has always been amazing to me that the Labour Government did not attempt to nationalise it.'[3]

Nationalise Labour finally did, in 1947. The Electricity Act of that year had set up a number of area selling boards. In addition it had created a British Electricity Authority (BEA), later known as the Central Electricity Authority (CEA), with the double duty of generating electrical power to be distributed to the area boards and of exercising a 'general control' over their policy. The Herbert Committee judged this double duty to be too much and to be responsible in part for a slowness in the construction of generating stations, though that is a debatable point. Accordingly it recommended, alongside the area selling boards, a separate Generating Board and a new independent body charged with the duty of supervising the industry. In particular the new independent body was to possess a power of direction, over, for example, capital expenditure programmes, subject to confirmation by the Minister.

There lay the rub. All nationalisation statutes give the Minister a power of direction over the relevant industry, to be exercised, however, only in the general or national interest. Not once, to my knowledge, has the power been invoked, largely, I imagine, because the problem of giving directions has arisen in specific cases, difficult to reconcile with the 'national interest', whatever that might mean. Here, however, was a recommendation to the effect that the power of direction be exercised by a subordinate body, subject to consultation with the Minister. This would have implied an enormous departure

---

[1]   T. G. N. Haldane, Papers, Archives Centre, Churchill Collège, Cambridge.
[2]   Leslie Hannah, *Electricity before Nationalisation*, Macmillan, London, 1979, p. 37.   [3]   Ibid., p. 89.

from accepted ministerial practice. If the Minister were to acquiesce in this direction, he would be a cipher. If, on the other hand, he were to disagree, he would need his own monitoring staff, duplicating that of the new independent body. There were the makings here of friction between the new supervising body and the Ministry. This alone put the proposal out of court, though no member of the Herbert Committee seems to have taken the point.

What then to do? One could go either in favour of a more centralised system or for complete decentralisation. My mind was fairly evenly balanced. Various considerations inclined me, however, towards complete decentralisation. There was the tenor of the Herbert Report itself; there was the hostility, justified or unjustified, expressed against the chairman of the CEA, Lord Citrine, allegedly on grounds of over-centralisation; there was the mood of the Conservative back-benchers; above all there was the Ministry's experience with the gas industry, in which each Area Board was individually accountable to the Ministry. The Ministry's knowledge of the gas industry was as a result greater than that of any other industry falling within its ambit.

Accordingly I plumped for an organisation akin to that of the Gas Council – an Electricity Council, comprising the generating board, the selling boards, and a trio of independent members on whose advice I could rely. The point of the organisation was to render each Board accountable. Citrine implored me to make him chairman of the new Council. Aged 70, he was mentally alert and I had nothing against him. He stood, however, for a system which I was trying to change, and his occupancy of the new office would have made others feel that there was no change. I had therefore, as nicely as I could, to say 'No'. My successor appointed, as chairman of the Council, Sir Henry Self, Citrine's deputy, with Citrine as a part-time member. To my mind even this was placing the new authority under the old guard, and thus reinforcing the tendency to conservatism. It was only after four years that Sir Ronald Edwards, a member of the Herbert Committee, became chairman of the Council; in evidence to the House of Commons Select Committee on Nationalised Industries (Vol. 1, Chapter 1), he considered that in spite of earlier views, the Council's statutory powers were adequate and the committee itself concluded that the structure of the industry was sound.

All organisations are, however, impermanent, and later generations believed that there should be a change. A further committee of enquiry was set up under Lord Plowden. It came to conclusions different from mine.[4] But it was never acted on. It ran counter in particular to the instincts of the then Minister, Mr Benn, a fact which Lord Plowden should have known, or at least made it his business to know. But whether he was knowledgeable or not, the report went down the drain. There is no point in any outside committee unless its report is followed by action. Such action I was determined to secure, and to secure it I had to face Rab Butler.

Butler presided over the Home Affairs Committee of the Cabinet, before which all projected legislation passed. He instructed me to sound out the views of the back-benchers' Fuel and Power Committee. I did so, and the views were cordial. On reporting back, I was instructed to appear again before the back-benchers' Fuel and Power Committee, presumably with a view to making assurance doubly sure. Even with a further favourable report, Butler was still not satisfied.[5]

Finally we went to the Cabinet with two opposing papers. As I remember it, he feared that the reorganisation of the electricity industry might lead to a demand for the reorganisation of other nationalised industries. There would in fact have been nothing untoward in reviewing the organisation of other nationalised industries. In addition he thought that back-benchers might be upset because I had failed to act on one particular Herbert recommendation – namely, that selling boards should go to the capital market without a Treasury guarantee.

This was not a recommendation on which anybody could have possibly acted, the Chancellor, Mr Macmillan, having, in his budget of the spring 1956, laid it down that all financial advances to nationalised industries should be through the Treasury. The purpose of this provision was to facilitate the management of Government debt, the issue always uppermost in the Treasury's mind over and above the efficiency of the nationalised industries. I countered with the opinion that the Suez debacle required an acceleration of the nuclear power programme, and this in its turn required a streamlined Generating Board. I was supported by Lord Salisbury who, as President of the Council, held responsibilities for nuclear power and was advised by

[4]   Structure of Electricity Supply Industry in England and Wales, Cmnd. 6388, 1976.
[5]   'Butler had the utmost difficulty in making up his mind', Lord Roberthall, British Oral Archives of Political and Administrative History, British Library of Political and Economic Science.

Lord Plowden, chairman of the Atomic Energy Authority (AEA). I won, but was the victory of avail?

The decision to embark on the development of nuclear power for military purposes had been taken in 1947, though somewhat half-heartedly. For civil purposes the decision was taken in the spring of 1952, when the Government gave its approval to a long-term programme, including the building of a fast or breeder reactor, which could ultimately dispense with the need for exhaustible uranium. In the summer, however, the military chiefs were demanding more plutonium for military purposes, this demand causing a diversion of attention from the civil programme. So disturbing was this diversion that Sir Christopher (later Lord) Hinton, head of the industrial branch of the AEA, concluded that there was no certainty that a reactor for civil purposes would be approved.

Before my arrival on the scene my predecessor had, in spite of all the doubts, announced in February 1955, a first nuclear power programme – 12 stations to be built by 1965, contributing in total 6 per cent of the estimated total energy needs of the United Kingdom, a proportion prophesied to rise to 15–20 per cent by 1975. Among the enthusiasts was the late Dr Bronowski, Director of the National Coal Board's Central Research Establishment. 'The programme', he said, 'is modest.'[6]

The only sceptical voice that I then knew of was that of Sir Harold Hartley, who, in his capacity as chairman of the OEEC Commission on Energy, said: 'Atomic power is not just round the corner . . . There is still a danger of wishful thinking about this new source of power.'[7]

Subsequently I learned that Lord Hinton also had his doubts. Nonetheless I persuaded him to accept the chairmanship of the Central Electricity Generating Board, though it was my successor who confirmed the appointment. In later life he felt he had been a failure in the appointment, and that he should have been made member of the Board for Engineering. Certainly, as chairman of the CEGB he gave the impression of having become more hesitant over nuclear power, though even his earlier speeches betray a note of caution.

He rightly prophesied that the first nuclear reactor in the world to generate electrical power for civil purposes would be Calder Hall in

---

[6] Dr J. Bronowski, Lecture to the Association of Mining, Electrical and Mechanical Engineers, York, 28 October 1955.
[7] Hartley Papers, Archives Centre, Churchill College, Cambridge.

Cumbria. Started in mid-1953, it was completed by October 1956. I well remember the opening ceremony. Britain had been the country which started the first Industrial Revolution; now she was starting the second. Such was the conversation on the train to Cumberland.

The enthusiasm was misplaced and put subsequent British nuclear development on a wrong track. Way back in 1946, the technology talked of had been different. Then it had been envisaged that uranium, having undergone purification, would be used as the raw material (or core) of the pile, with graphite to moderate its explosive power and water as a coolant. Water, however, absorbs neutrons more easily than graphite, the moderator, so that if there were a loss of water, the excess of neutrons then available might make the pile unstable.

Accordingly a switch was made to the use of carbon dioxide as the coolant, a less powerful absorber of neutrons than the moderator, the reactor pile thus being rendered more stable. This was the technology embodied in Calder Hall and in the reactors (known as Magnox) based on it – purified uranium heated to a high intensity with a resulting fission of the atomic nucleus, and with graphite to moderate the force of the fission, and gas to act as a coolant.

It is possible that this technology was common at that time to all three nuclear powers – the United States, the United Kingdom and the Soviet Union. At a date difficult to determine, however, the United States swerved in a different direction. Pushed by the active Admiral Rickover, who wanted a nuclear powered submarine, the Americans contrived a different process: enriched uranium as the raw material, with little need for a moderator, and water as the coolant. From the seas this technology was transferred to the land, the Tennessee Valley Authority, for example, placing an order at a capital cost at that time slightly cheaper than that of a power station fired by fossil fuels – though the capital cost has since risen sharply. Already the American model was beginning to capture the imagination of the rest of the world.

Meanwhile in a Britain fired by the success of Calder Hall and convinced of the rightness of its technology, there was a mounting pressure to proceed faster. The pressure came from diverse quarters: public opinion, politicians frightened by the Suez war, and the 'enthusiasm of research teams without industrial responsibility.'[8] In Hinton's

8   Hinton, speech to a post-graduate seminar at the London School of Economics, 31 January 1961; Hinton Papers, Archives Centre, Churchill College, Cambridge.

opinion, it was a mistake to continue shock tactics after Calder Hall.[9]

If this was indeed Hinton's view at the time, his was a lone voice. The only question for nearly everybody was whether the programme announced in 1955 should now be doubled, trebled, or even quadrupled. Official historians have assumed that the decision lay with me, the Minister of Fuel and Power. The assumption, however, rests on an ignorance of the machinery of government. Matters of moment are not decided on by a single Minister. Recommendations gravitate up to him through a hierarchy of inter-Departmental officials.

I have always held that a competent Minister can be in effective charge of matters within his own Department. All important matters, however, straddle a range of Departments. An inter-Departmental committee of officials is then set up. Often such a committee is necessary; sometimes it is not, being due to the reluctance of the Cabinet to take a difficult decision. Whatever the origin, however, of an inter-Departmental committee of officials, the collectivity of officials will prevail over the collectivity of Ministers. Even though one Minister may wish to disagree, he may be sure that his ministerial colleagues will accept the officials' recommendations. In one case I know of a Minister, member of a Cabinet sub-committee considering recommendations from an inter-Departmental committee of officials, was transferred from one Department to another. He then changed tack, supporting, against his previous views, the recommendations of his new officials. He was subsequently highly promoted.

In the case of nuclear power there was a committee comprising representatives of the Ministry, the Treasury, the CEA, the AEA, and doubtless other Departments. The official view of the AEA was that the programme could be safely trebled, a view communicated to me in a private letter by Sir Edwin (later Lord) Plowden. Sir John Cockcroft, head of research at the AEA, on the other hand, expressed to me in conversation the view that the programme could be quadrupled. Clearly the technologists were being held back by the administrators. A reverse process was taking place in the CEA. Lord Citrine, the administrator, was all for accelerating the programme; Mr (later Sir) Josiah Eccles, the engineer, on the other hand, was placing a restraining hand. The summary recommendation was that the programme should be trebled. No Minister could have gone against a recommen-

9 Ibid.

dation of such authority. Fortunately, it did not fall to me to pronounce upon it. The relevant statement was made to the public by my successor, Lord Mills. But I myself would have taken exactly the same decision, wrong in retrospect though it would have been.

Indeed I had penned, though not submitted, a Cabinet paper based on a letter which I had sent to the Prime Minister on 7 December 1956. I had then said that the AEA were of the opinion that technological advance would permit a quadrupling of the programme and had taken steps to ensure that the requisite raw materials were available. They felt, however, that this would be a crash action. Prudence would seem to indicate trebling as a minimum, with an undertaking to keep the situation constantly under review so that further improvements could be made in later years if possible and desirable. The course of caution thus recommended turned out in fact to be one of profligacy.

6

NUCLEAR POWER

The trebling of the nuclear power programme in the second half of the 1950s was estimated to raise the contribution of nuclear power to the total energy requirements of the country to around 6 per cent in 1965 and to 15–20 per cent in 1975. In 1982 the nuclear contribution was 5.1 per cent on a coal equivalent basis as compared with roughly equal shares of coal and oil – 35.3 and 35.6 per cent.[1] This was one of the lowest nuclear contributions to the supply of energy in the Western world, certainly well below France and Scandinavia (see Appendix 3). Not only did coal output decline, but the nuclear output also fell far short of expectations. What went wrong?

Lord Hinton put the problem graphically: 'We started four war-time years behind them [the USA]; after only ten years we had a lead of at least two years. It took only another seven years to throw that lead away.'[2]

There are several explanations for the loss of lead. There were, for example, the never-ending cuts in public spending. Scarcely was the trebling of the programme announced than the Treasury succeeded in deferring the output targetted by a year – the 6,000 or so MW to be attained in 1966 rather than in 1965, with the implication that the target for 1965 was now reduced to little more than 5,000 MW.

There was the accident at Windscale, now renamed Sellafield, in 1957, when a fire was discovered in some of the reactor channels, causing a release of radioactivity. This was a worse accident than that which occurred later at Three Mile Island, in the United States, an accident due in large part to inexperienced management. A military reactor, Windscale released 20,000 curies of iodine; Three Mile Island, a reactor for civil purposes, released only 30 curies of iodine. The Windscale accident had not been entirely unforeseen. The reaction in the pile was moderated by graphite. Under the bombardment of neut-

[1] *Digest of UK Energy Statistics*, 1983.
[2] Lord Hinton, Memoirs Archives Centre, Churchill College, Cambridge.

rons, however, the atomic structure of graphite changes its shape and dimension. This effect had led to an accident at Hanford in the United States in the late 1940s. It had almost led to an accident at Windscale in 1951–3. In vain Hinton pleaded with Harwell, the AEA Research Centre, to investigate the phenomenon, known, after an American of Hungarian origin, as the Wigner phenomenon. Little, if anything, however, had been done to deepen the understanding of the problem. Then there took place the occurrence of 1957. 'We had continually asked for a better charting of the Wigner area . . . At last we had gambled with the gods for too long and had hit the rock that we had asked to be thoroughly charted.'[3] Subsequently the charting was thoroughly done, though it is questionable whether it was carried quite far enough.

The main accident at Windscale apart, there had also been some minor incidents, incidents which have continued to this day. In the autumn of 1955 a physicist on the Windscale staff complained that he had found specks of plutonium on the cabbages in his garden. Hinton admitted: 'It is quite possible I was to blame for it.'[4] He attributed the incident to filters which had been placed on the chimney pot to prevent the emission of particles, but 'I had been suggesting for some time that their removal might be considered,'[5] provided this could be safely done. They reduced output and increased cost. 'After an exhaustive search . . . the health physicists in the district monitoring team did find traces of particulate activity elsewhere.'[6] Whether in the event the filters were removed is not clear.

In addition a few cases had been discovered of slight over-exposure of process operators, but with one exception the men were merely put off duty for a few weeks or, very occasionally, a few months. The one exception (in 1952) was that of an instrument mechanic whose hands were found to be contaminated when he monitored them as he came off shift. Re-scrubbing failed to remove the radiation activity and when he reported to the works surgery the following day it was found that he was contaminated with plutonium liquor. So also was his house. This remains the worst case of this kind yet encountered. Hinton's account, written some 30 years after the event, does not accord with the facts. The facts appear to be that the man was endeavouring to clear a blocked pipe; and in the process he became badly contaminated with plutonium liquor. By and large, however, Hinton had been tremendously proud of the safety record of the AEA's Industrial Group.

The effect of the main Windscale accident was to cause a considerable re-design of the cores at Bradwell and Berkely (the first Magnox reactors) and to delay the introduction of a new type of reactor, the Advanced Gas Cooled Reactor (AGR). Whereas the forecast had been that electricity generated at Bradwell and Berkely would cost around 0.6 pence per kilowatt hour (kWh), the cost was in fact doubled to one penny per kWh. In spite of this initial setback, the generating costs of other Magnox reactors (Dungeness 'A', Sizewell 'A', Hinkley Point 'A', Oldbury, Trawsfynydd and Wylfa) turned out to be similar to that of coal: Magnox 2.06 pence per kWh, coal 2.05 pence and oil 3.22 pence.[7]

After Windscale there was little hope of developing the Magnox reactor to a point at which it would be truly economical. A different design had to be developed. In spite of his doubts about graphite when subjected to extreme conditions Hinton went for another graphite-moderated reactor – the AGR. The puzzle is why. Conventional power stations had been able to lower their costs through their ability to achieve high temperatures. Comparable temperatures could be obtained, in Hinton's belief, only in a graphite-moderated gas-cooled reactor. Water-cooled reactors, though more compact, could not generate such high temperatures. The decision therefore was in favour of an AGR, the first to be constructed at Dungeness and designated Dungeness 'B' to distinguish it from the Magnox reactor, Dungeness 'A'.

Dungeness 'B' proved to be a disaster. There were considerable delays in construction, delays which allowed the United States to take the market lead. These could be attributed in part to continual changes of design, in part to a lack of familiarity with nuclear power on the part of the contracting consortium. There was also a problem with labour. Navvies building railways in the nineteenth century were a mobile team. The team constructing Dungeness 'B' was an established local community, anxious to prolong the work.

As originally conceived, nuclear power was to be used for weapon purposes only. It seemed logical, therefore, to locate it in the Ministry of Supply, the Department responsible within Government for the provision of engines of war. Firms, however, were already turning

---

[7]   *Analysis of Generation Costs*, Central Electricity Generating Board.

their minds to exports and displayed little interest in nuclear power for military uses.

Accordingly the development of nuclear power, both for military and civil purposes was transferred to a 'quango', the AEA, it being considered that an independent Authority could contrive greater flexibility and decentralisation than a Government Department. The British AEA however, had wider tasks than its American counterpart, the US Atomic Energy Commission. The latter formulated policy and directed operations, while leaving to private firms, research, design and construction. The British organisation, by contrast, undertook most of its own research work and virtually all of its own design, construction and the operation of establishments. It was under this all-embracing organisation that Calder Hall was built.

The AEA was a unique institution, even in a surrounding world which stubbornly remained uniquely British. 'Research and engineering achieved an authority and standing which was felt to be higher than the operations branch. This is contrary to the position in process industries . . . where in general (and equally undesirably) the operations branch has the higher authority.'[8] There was as a result a degree of difficulty in recruiting operating staff and too rapid a promotion of those recruited; this was one of the causes of the delay in the execution of the programme.

With the trebling of the programme, the AEA could clearly not accomplish all itself; it therefore had to farm out. It found itself, however, in the same problem as the Ministry of Supply before it – firms were reluctant to come forward. Perhaps they were informed enough to be put off by American experience. As Mr Weaver, the president of the Atomic Power Division of the Westinghouse Electrical Corporation, put it: 'It was the toughest job we ever took on – harder by far than jet engine research . . . We hope no-one will underestimate the difficulties of developing and building a large power reactor. Such a miscalculation could produce a blow to hope and progress.'[9]

In spite of this trans-Atlantic warning the Government proceeded to entrust its expanded programme to four consortia of electrical engineering firms, the contracts being allotted by tender. The four

[8]   Lord Hinton, post-graduate seminar at the London School of Economics, 31 January 1961, Hinton Papers, Archives Centre, Churchill College, Cambridge.
[9]   Lord Hinton, Clayton Memorial Lecture, 26 February 1954, Hinton Papers, Archives Centre, Churchill College, Cambridge.

consortia seemed to come into being of their own accord rather than as a result of a decision of the Ministry of Fuel and Power. To whomever the responsibility belonged, the decision was clearly mistaken. It ignored the essential fact – that the potential national demand was too small for four consortia, so that one or other of them had at some stage to carry only a half-load.

The structure created in Britain contrasts with the policy followed both in the United States and in France. The market for nuclear power in the United States was ten times as large as that in the United Kingdom. While there were, as in the United Kingdom, four suppliers, each had ten times as much business as its British counterpart.[10] In France, with a somewhat larger market for nuclear power than the United Kingdom, a standardised design was drawn up for all nuclear stations, with single suppliers for all key items. Competition may be a virtue in a large economy; in a small economy it may make nonsense.

The nonsense became only too clear in the United Kingdom. There was 'a proliferation of different designs each with its own teething troubles, none of the advantages of [repeated orders], major components inadequately tested through lack of funds and development work and remedial work having to be carried out as the construction progressed'.[11] The fault lay not with the electricity industry, which 'was alert and progressive in its technological thinking',[12] but with the structure resulting from competitive firms. Not a single consortium seems to have foreseen that with the increasing size of a plant which was economic (it is now 1,000 MW as compared with the initial 200MW) and with an economy which could turn (and has turned) stagnant, it would not be able to supply the small increments in demand required. The consortia were reduced to two; and the two subsequently to one – the National Nuclear Corporation.

Hinton himself was highly critical of the firms. 'The commercial business of designing and building nuclear power plants was handed over to industrial firms in 1956; these industrial firms have failed to contribute to our national prosperity.'[13]

Apart from the problem of too many unschooled firms there was

[10] Sir John Hill, Wilson Campbell Lecture, 14 March 1983.
[11] Ibid.
[12] Lord Hinton, post-graduate seminar at London School Economics, 31 January 1961, Hinton Papers, Archives Centre, Churchill College, Cambridge.
[13] Lord Hinton, Memoirs, Archives Centre, Churchill College, Cambridge.

also present, in a more pronounced degree than before, a new problem –
the gulf between the scientist and the engineer. Possibly that gulf may
have existed since the days of Charles II, when the Royal Society,
which was science-orientated, was founded. It was now widened.

Design consists of two principal stages. The earlier stage of the concept, the lay-out and the arrangement of the plant needs to be undertaken by individuals with a high level of academic training. The
subsequent stage consists of the detailed design of the machinery and
the equipment.

Under the pre-war educational system the second stage was undertaken by an apprentice straight from school; he could, however,
graduate to the first stage – that of framing the concept. Under the
post-war system of education this progression has been broken. The
potential designer now goes straight to the university; he then
embarks on a two-year post-graduate apprenticeship. By this time he
is too sophisticated to communicate easily with the craftsman, and the
intimate relationship that used to exist between the designer and the
craftsman is destroyed. Hinton differed strongly from Lord Robbins;
he himself had begun life in a factory, accordingly he believed that
design could be taught only in design offices, not in universities, and
that a university course needed to be preceded by workshop
training.[14]

The first successor to the Magnox reactors, AGR, at Dungeness suffered experiences similar to the Magnox. It was slow to complete, the
resulting delays, with the attendant increase in capital costs, ruling it
out of the world market. Had it been completed on time Hinton was
convinced that the British AGR would have competed successfully
against American designs. The delays were not true of subsequent
AGRs, but the world had already decided on the reactor it wanted –
the American Pressurised Water Reactor (PWR). He who would compete in the world has no option but to follow the world's fashion. This
the CEGB finally did, deciding in favour of a PWR reactor located at
Sizewell. Its hand had been forced by an unsuited industrial structure
and by the gulf between the scientists of the AEA and the engineers in
industry who were required to conform with their demands.

It was British Nuclear Fuels, a development of the Production Division of the AEA, engaged in the reprocessing of spent fuels, which first

[14] Lord Hinton, Presidential Address to British Electrical Power Convention, 17 June
1963, Hinton Papers, Archives Centre, Churchill College, Cambridge.

perceived the need for catering for a world market. Forming a partnership with Japan and other Western European countries, it became an organisation which transcended the confines of the United Kingdom and was the first nuclear entity to escape from the uniqueness of being British.

Why, given all the subsequent delays, were we all so keen to expedite the nuclear power programme? Market signals in the sense of price scarcely entered into it. The estimated operating costs of nuclear and conventional power stations were almost equal – 0.66 pence for a nuclear station, given a reactor life of 20 years; and between 0.52 and 0.64 pence for a conventional station. The speed with which the cost of conventional power was reduced upset this calculation. An important difference lay in the capital cost – that of a nuclear station amounting to twice to three times that of a conventional station. In spite of the increased capital cost Sir Josiah Eccles, deputy chairman of the CEA, in a letter to me agreed to the trebling of the initial programme.

The cardinal consideration, however, was not price or even capital cost, but the benefits which could be foreseen for the balance of payments. The estimated need for energy in 1965 was 320 million tons of coal equivalent (mtce). The target for coal output – unlikely to be reached – was 240–250 million tons. Without the roughly 20 million tons of coal which it was thought could be saved by the enhanced nuclear power programme, oil imports would have to be increased beyond the projected 80 million tons of coal equivalent. Even then we would as a country be consuming over 50 per cent more oil than in 1955.

In sum, the decision to go ahead with nuclear power was based on the political uncertainties of oil supplies from the Middle East and the extremely dubious projections of British coal output. In December 1956 I drafted a paper on the subject for the Cabinet; this was never submitted because of my removal from the scene. It was an elaboration of a paper which I had already sent to the Prime Minister. The considerations I put forward still stand 30 years later. We need diversity of sources for supplies of basic fuel; otherwise we are at risk.

But are we at risk from nuclear power? In a sense there is always a risk. What matters is the adequacy of safety devices to deal instantly with anything that might go wrong. That depends both on the CEGB and on the Nuclear Inspectorate. The main risk from nuclear power – though it is the risk least talked about – is the release of radioactivity from an untoward happening in the reactor. This risk is vanishingly small; to cope with it quick-acting devices are needed to close down the reactor. This has not happened to the 20 or so civil reactors operating in this country. The outstanding example of this particular risk was the accident at Three Mile Island, in the United States. Though there was no release of radioactivity, that accident has brought the American nuclear power programme practically to a standstill.

The danger most talked about is that which might arise from nuclear waste. It is a lesser danger, since contamination from nuclear waste is slow acting and can be dealt with at minimal cost. The waste can be kept on site, vitrified and sealed, or it can be deposited in suitable geological structures, the best being a clay pit, since it cannot be subject to distortion of the rock through earth tremors or glaciation. Although the risk is small, the public fear is great. In France this fear has been dealt with through a scheme of special discounts to inhabitants in the neighbourhood of nuclear power stations. In this country the fact of resort to a foreign reactor – the PWR – has probably enhanced the fear and has led to the protracted enquiry into the projected PWR reactor at Sizewell. There is no point in just one PWR reactor; the contracting industry requires a programme ahead. Such a programme will not be possible if every projected PWR reactor is subjected to a similar lengthy enquiry. The nuclear power industry will die, and with it the prospect in the next century of power generated by fast reactors, which are miniscule in their demand for uranium. On both technical and economic grounds, fusion can be ruled out for at least a century.

If the industry is indeed to die, there would be a case for joining hands with the French and the Germans in developing the fast reactor, this being a safeguard against the exhaustion of uranium. A joint company with France, Britain countributing 20 per cent, is in fact under consideration. The United Kingdom has an experimental fast reactor at Dounreay, but has not proceeded further. France, by contrast, has, in addition to the experimental fast reactor (Phenix), advanced to the construction and, I believe, demonstration of a commercial fast reactor (super Phenix).

The French electricity industry, having set itself a target of 80 per cent as the nuclear contribution to the need for electrical power, a target modified in 1983 to 40–50 per cent, because of the recession, has achieved a lower cost per kWh than its British counterpart. The difference is probably of the order of 25–30 per cent. France has overtaken us in the nuclear field, as she has in others, and in terms of energy has equipped French industry to compete successfully against manufacturing industries elsewhere.

It is evident that the future of nuclear power in the United Kingdom is highly uncertain. This is not a question of the market – nuclear power would undoubtedly make electricity much cheaper. What is at issue now is public acceptability. Such evidence as there is suggests that the more the issue is debated, the less acceptable does nuclear power become; the Sizewell inquiry indeed may have had a perverse effect. 'Privatisation' is irrelevant in this context. It is possible indeed that an attempt to 'privatise', in whatever form, might weaken the attempt to convince public opinion that nuclear power can be 'safe'. It might be considered unwise to leave the manufacture of a product considered dangerous to private hands. It is safety, not ownership, which, over the years, has now become the dominant question.

If the public can be satisfied on the issue of safety, then nuclear civil reactors located within reach of large cities, could give supplies of heat as well as generate power. This was always possible with smaller generating stations. The problem is considerably greater with the larger stations now required to produce power economically. Nonetheless Sir Walter Marshall, in evidence to the Select Committee on Energy, gave this opinion: 'I believe it is economically worthwhile... I also have to say that the problems of implementing it and launching it are very difficult. I think the problems of marketing it are formidable.'[15] There, for the time being, the matter has to be left.

[15] House of Commons Select Committee on Energy, 2 December 1982, HMSO, p. 36.

7
GAS

Like coal and electricity, gas, then based on the carbonisation of coal, was also a fragmented industry – over 1,200 undertakings before nationalisation. Some were small, some large, though differences in size were not necessarily reflected in differences in financial performance. The main determinant of size was technology; 'it was not practicable to transmit relatively small quantities of gas over long distances; it was better to convey coal to small local works'.[1] This multiplicity of undertakings led, among other results, to confusion for the consumer. 'Appliances might be available in one supply area on terms quite different from those offered in another only a few miles away.'[2] More important, there was an absence of research, a defect remedied only when Sir Harold Hartly joined the board of the largish Gas Light and Coal Company and ultimately became head of the research laboratory of Watson House, its facilities being made available to other companies on subscription.

It was the extension of the role of gas from lighting to heating, particularly industrial heating, that precipitated reorganisation. The new role put gas into competition with electricity, already undergoing co-ordination, and coal producing gas as a by-product of coke. The nationalisation of coal was on the horizon long before 1945. How could a dispersed industry like gas effectively buy coke from a single coal industry? The projected nationalisation of coal thus presaged the nationalisation of gas. This was seen by a war-time committee under Mr Geoffrey (later Lord) Heyworth, which advocated 'the compulsory purchase of all existing undertakings, and the subsequent division of the country into ten regions, each under a regional board consisting of a chairman and six directors. All directors would be appointed by the Minister . . .' All this uncompromisingly amounted to public ownership.[3] All that a Labour Government had to do

[1] Trevor I. Williams, *A History of the British Gas Industry*, Oxford University Press, 1981, p. 70. [2] Ibid., p. 34 [3] Ibid., p. 96.

therefore was to build on grounds, set for it for pragmatic reasons, by a private industrialist.

Organisational change was not to end with nationalisation. New processes were developed which generated gas at high pressure and thus made possible the construction of an integrated grid system similar to that in electricity. In these changed circumstances the area boards which I inherited had no need to manufacture; they could depend on the grid. Thus technology once again pushed power towards the centre. This shift of power was symbolised after my time by the Gas Act of 1965, which gave a power to manufacture gas to the Gas Council, comprising all the area boards with some independent members.

Even during my tenure at the Ministry of Fuel and Power the straight conversion of natural gas into gas for domestic and industrial purposes had been foreseen, and plans were being drawn up for the import of methane from Algeria. With the later discovery of natural gas in the North Sea the reliance of the industry on coal and coke ceased. The concentration of power at the centre became complete, a Gas Corporation coming into being with the passage of an act by a Conservative Government in 1972, the area boards finally disappearing from the scene.

Would the transformation of the industry have taken place at the rate it did without nationalisation? The answer must clearly be speculative. Trevor I. Williams cites Tawney as having written: 'Its [nationalisation's] success depends . . . not on the mere change of ownership, but on the degree to which advantage is taken of the opportunity offered by it to secure first-class management, to carry through measures of re-organisation which private enterprise was unable or unwilling to undertake.'[4] Certainly the gas industry, in spite of the relative smallness of the initial undertaking, ultimately secured first-class management, as did the electricity industry, in the shape of Sir Ronald Edwards. It is equally true that in its fragmented state the industry was unable or unwilling to carry through reorganisation. Finally it was the existence of a central body made possible by nationalisation which facilitated an extensive research and development programme. It is the threat to research and development which would be the greatest danger arising from a possible break-up of the industry through 'privatisation'.

It must have been this kind of transformation which Mr Richard

[4]   Ibid., p. 241.

Pryke must have had in mind when he wrote: 'the conclusion seems irresistible that the technical efficiency of the public enterprise has been rising more rapidly than that of the private sector, and that this must in part have been due to the way in which it is organised and managed'.[5]

In a later book Mr Pryke was more critical of the nationalised industries in general, but less so of gas.[6] 'The performance of the nationalised industries over the past decade has ranged from being good in parts –. . . gas – to being almost wholly bad.' Again, 'The productivity performance of gas . . . seems excellent.'[7] What he appears to have had in mind is the quiet disappearance of workers from gasworks as North Sea gas came on stream. The main criticisms which he appears to have had in mind is the low price paid by the Gas Corporation, as the authorised single buyer, for gas from the southern part of the North Sea and (in his view) the unnecessarily low prices initially charged to consumers. Later, when the Corporation had to pay a market price for gas from the northern part of the North Sea, where drilling was deeper and costs were therefore higher, prices were renegotiated upwards.[8]

The nationalised gas industry reached its peak in the 1972 Act. The central purpose of this act was to reinforce the power of the Gas Corporation, in particular to negotiate long-term contracts with oil companies for gas from the North Sea, to develop a depletion policy, and to run a national transmission system with a national sales policy. That act entrusted the Gas Corporation with two main functions: (1) to search and bore for and get natural gas; (2) to bore for and get petroleum found in the form of crude oil as a result of its searching, boring and getting. The two functions are related, since gas and oil are frequently, though not invariably, found in combination. (They are, for example, dissociated in the southern part of the North Sea.) How far had the industry, up to this point, been acting in accordance with Mr Lawson's dictum of operating in a freely competitive market? There are at least two respects in which it had not. First, the extraction of natural gas from the North Sea was delayed (or rather the authorities acquiesced in engineering delays)[9] in order to uphold the demand for

[5]   Richard Pryke, *Public Enterprise in Practice*, MacGibbon and Kee, London, 1971, p. 436.
[6]   Richard Pryke, *The Nationalised Industries, Policies and Performance since 1968*, Martin Robertson, Oxford University Press, 1981.   [7] Ibid., p. 257.
[8]   Ibid., p. 242.
[9]   Cf. Michael V. Posner, *Fuel Policy*, Macmillan, London, 1973, p. 309.

coal. Secondly, the market price for gas had to reflect the excise duty on fuel oil introduced in 1962. Clearly there was no statutory duty on the gas industry to price its production this way, and one can only presume that there must have been ministerial pressure, again to maintain the demand for coal. As a result the competitive power of gas was doubly restricted.

Gas supplies in the North Sea are likely to continue to be available until around the turn of the century. Plans are already under way to import gas from other countries, for example, Norway. When the North Sea gas reserves are exhausted, there will be no alternative but to look elsewhere. The most expensive source open to the Gas Corporation would be to resort again to the importation of liquefied natural gas from Algeria. The import of coal from South Africa would in fact be cheaper. And perhaps it is as well to remember that in Northern Ireland gas is produced from oil. So long, however, as the source of gas is the North Sea the important question is whether the known reserves should be rapidly depleted or not. Mr Pryke, in his later volume, opines that the Gas Corporation 'is pursuing a policy which is basically correct, namely a strategy of conserving the reserves in the southern part of the North Sea and placing maximum reliance on the northern sector'.[10] This statement contradicts the assertion cited earlier that the price of gas from the southern part of the North Sea is being kept too low. The only way of conserving a depletable source is ultimately to raise the price. However, he adds: 'It would be . . . wrong at a time when . . . the demand for gas is very high to restrict supplies if the price which consumers are prepared to pay exceeds the extraction and depletion cost of southern gas.'[11] Economically wrong? Morally wrong? And how does one assess 'depletion cost'? The statement is unclear. All one can say is that the maximisation of short-term profit is not necessarily appropriate for a public corporation which might well have a long-term interest in retarding the depletion of gas.

It is the policy of Mrs Thatcher's Government to sell to the public the oil interests acquired by the Gas Corporation under the 1972 act. This is an ill reward for service well done; the gas industry was in my experience the most efficient of the nationalised industries under my jurisdiction; and to deprive it of an accomplishment is not calculated to attract talent to publicly owned industries.

[10] Pryke, *The Nationalised Industries*, p. 21. [11] Ibid.

Worse, it largely deprives the Government of the power to regulate the rate at which a scarce resource is depleted. The main power of regulation which the Government theoretically has is to control the rate at which it issues licences for exploration or alternatively invites bids at an auction. If the area for which licences are issued is smaller than the known reserves, then the theoretical power to regulate the rate of depletion becomes indeed real. The likelihood, however, is that licences will be issued for the whole of the fields then known. The regulation of the issue of licences can be complemented by a power to specify production levels when permission to develop a field is granted. Unless this power is exercised, the rate of depletion then depends on the oil companies, in so far as they produce gas in association with oil. There are some economists who hold that oil companies, for it is they who are the likely purchasers of the Gas Corporation's oil interests, balance the present against the future rate of extraction according to their view of future prices. For my part, I remain a sceptic. It is in human nature to pay greater attention to the known present than to the unknown future, and to make profit now while rivals are making profit. If this is so, competitive market forces are likely to accelerate the rate of depletion, the last thing which a country which underwent the oil crisis arising from the Suez war of 1956 should wish to do. In other words, oil companies will act as the Government has acted – grab what they can. Indeed the Government is already experiencing this. Having changed its mind and having come round in favour of retarded depletion, it finds itself unable to enforce its will.

Finally, there is the question of the Government's influence on price. In a white paper of 1967 the Government laid it down that prices should reflect the long-term cost of raising increments of output. An investigation by the National Economic Development Office revealed that few, if any, nationalised industries had any exact idea of the long-term incremental cost. Accordingly, the Government, or, strictly speaking the Treasury, without formally abandoning the principle of relating prices to the cost of raising output in the long term, in effect substituted for it in practice a specified rate of return on new investment. There were at least two practical reasons why the Treasury should seek from the Gas Corporation a higher rate of return. First, the Corporation was not paying any petroleum revenue tax on its finds in the southern part of the North Sea; it, rather than the Government, was therefore reaping the rent from a government-owned source. Secondly, when the profits of a nationalised corporation reach a certain level, corporation tax can be levied. Thus the Government has motives for raising the price of gas if for any reason it is deemed too low.

As a profitable nationalised industry gas is clearly a candidate for 'privatisation', even though it was nationalised precisely because of the defects of private ownership. One can only speculate about the form which 'privatisation' might take. For example, the national grid itself might be sold off to private shareholders. But given the probability of changes in the sources of gas, private investors seem unlikely to be attracted. For example, if British reserves in the North Sea were running low, production levels might be specified by the Government. Alternatively, if purchases of gas had to be made from elsewhere, for example, Norway or even Algeria, the negotiations over price would be subject to great uncertainty. Another option open to the Government would be to concentrate on selling, and breaking up the selling side of the Gas Corporation into the former dozen or so units or even a larger number. The difficulty with this course of action would be that capital and therefore operating costs would differ across the country. Wales, for instance, being thinly populated, would have higher costs than the neighbouring and more densely populated West Midlands. There are limits to the extent to which a democratically elected government can tolerate differences in the price charged to electors. Similar problems would arise in the case of electricity, if the 'privatisation' programme were confined to the selling side. The break-up of the grid itself seems scarcely conceivable.

The only clear case for 'privatisation' is in respect of showrooms. The sensible course of action is to do as the Herbert Committee recommended in the case of electricity – allow competition between private showrooms and Gas Corporation showrooms, provided that the latter show open accounts and the authorities rectify any inequalities in the competition.

If this line of reasoning is correct the Government will be forced to maintain an abridged mixed economy, like it or not, and deal with it with a degree of sympathy not so far shown.

8
OIL

Of the industries sponsored by the Ministry of Fuel and Power oil was the only one that was privately owned. Even that was subject to regulation in the United States, the regulation aiming at controlling production and thus indirectly controlling price. The alleged cartel of the 'Seven Sisters' or the seven major companies, which presumably had as its aim the control of production internationally, had already begun to break down. The first crack had appeared in the early 1950s with the nationalisation of the Iranian assets of the Anglo-Iranian Company, later BP. The settlement reached, to the best of my recollection, consisted in the establishment of a consortium comprising some oil companies – excluding BP – and the Iranian Government. Sir Anthony Eden subsequently wrote to me commenting that it had been a good arrangement. This event preceded my time and was of no immediate concern of mine. It is nonetheless surprising that the attempted nationalisation of Iranian oil was not seen to presage a similar move throughout the Middle East, with the control of the price of oil ultimately passing from the companies to governments. What did concern me then was the price at which oil was imported, there then being no knowledge of North Sea oil. All the evidence appeared to show that the low price – still absurdly based on the Mexican Gulf though the Arabian (Persian) Gulf was growing in importance – was favourable to the British balance of payments. With that I was content.

My contentment was, however, misplaced. The sandstorm which had made its first appearance in Iran at the beginning of the decade and which is still blowing strongly began to swirl in my direction in the spring of 1956. General Sir John Glubb, who had been chief of the general staff of the Arab Legion in Amman for 20 years, left Jordan in March of that year. From that moment it was clear that worse could follow, though to my knowledge the 'worse' was not then defined.

Preparations were immediately begun for oil rationing against the eventuality of hostilities. Stockpiling was out of the question, there being a shortage of tankers. The estimate of the reduction in oil supplies from the Middle East in the event of a short war was 25 per cent. That estimate proved accurate, partly with the aid of chance, for example, a mild winter in late 1956. However, I had no power to ration, this having been abolished in 1954. Nor was there any point in seeking renewal of the power while peace nominally reigned.

The prepared plan provided for an immediate reduction in oil supplies of 10 per cent, achieved by instructing the oil companies to cut by this percentage their deliveries to bulk customers and garages. In the view of the Federation of British Industries a reduction of this size would have no adverse effects on production. Later one would have to proceed to the larger reduction of 25 per cent. But this would require staff, using some crude method to allocate. No staff, however, was in being, and none could be recruited without powers.

The crisis finally broke on 26 July 1956, when the Suez Canal was nationalised by President Nasser of Egypt. On the following day the Cabinet decided to attempt to regain possession, if necessary by force. Sir Dermot Boyle, then Chief of the Air Force, asked the Prime Minister: 'May we, Sir, be allowed to use the atom bomb?' Whether the question was serious or facetious I do not know. I remember only that the entire Cabinet laughed. Perhaps that laugh was comment enough on the use of nuclear weaponry. The pursuance of the decision was remitted to the Egypt Committee and so passed out of my ken. The Israeli invasion of Egypt did not take place until three months later – 29 October 1956. And the first Anglo-French landings in Egypt occurred on 5 November 1956.

At the time of the Israeli invasion I was at Nottingham, dining with the local Electricity Board and on the following day opening a new coke oven plant. I learned of the invasion from the newspapers. At the celebratory lunch which followed the opening of the coke oven plant frantic calls came from London urging my return. I was returning anyhow. I needed powers to re-introduce rationing. I finally got them on 31 October 1956, more than six months after the preparation of the rationing plan.

The first phase – a reduction of 10 per cent – worked perfectly. The introduction of the second phase – the further reduction to 25 per cent – was accomplished in six weeks as against the estimated eight weeks.

Of as many as three and a half million applications expected under the second phase for additions over and above the official ration, only two million were received.

In technical terms the operation was therefore a success. But public opinion thought otherwise. Just as politicians, when confronted by a 'dictator' – and where is there not a dictator? – return in memory to the combination of Hitler and Mussolini, so public opinion returns to remembrances – the remembrance on this occasion of what was permitted in a protracted war – a low general allowance of oil with a large number of supplementary allowances. In fact, given the circumstances, and the prospect of a short war, the scheme now put forward was exactly and inevitably the opposite – a highish general allowance with as few supplementary allowances as possible.

The media hastened to pour forth their outrage. I was summoned to see Sir Anthony Eden, the Prime Minister. So also was the Parliamentary Secretary for the Ministry of Transport, the Minister being away. The trouble at Transport, responsible for the distribution of diesel, was far greater than at mine, responsible for the distribution of petrol and fuel oil. I found Anthony Eden, the Prime Minister, as always, perfectly understanding. It has been said of him that he interfered with Ministers. All I can say is that I never suffered any interference, and found that he intuitively grasped a situation and comprehended individuals far better than his successor, Mr Harold Macmillan.

At one sub-committee of the Cabinet, alarmed to a larger extent than the realities justified, Mr Macmillan suggested that an industrial tycoon be sent over to Texas to negotiate for increased oil supplies. I meekly suggested that it would be imprudent, if indeed practicable, to by-pass Washington, since the power of individual states of the US Federation to regulate production sprang ultimately from Washington. I was over-ruled and the suggestion of a direct approach to Texas was written into the minutes. Permanent Secretaries then had to put their heads together to rectify the minutes. There was no need to rectify anyway, the Texas Railroad Commission having decided on a further restriction of production, so that a mission to Texas would have been fruitless.

There remains the question: How did the Suez fiasco come about? There are some, at least two, plausible explanations. Eden and Dulles, the US Secretary of State, never hit it off, the first acting on instinct and the second given to long disquisitions which the first found unbearable. In addition, the American Administration was approaching an election; this fact appears never to have been fully grasped in Britain, not even by the Egypt Committee. After the election the US Administration acted more positively in the Middle East – witness, for example, the dispatch of troops to the Lebanon in 1958.

More important is the question of the long-term effect of Suez on the British economy. Clearly the exchange rate was adversely affected, and with it perhaps long-term confidence in the British currency. As far as industry was directly concerned, however, the effect was temporary. When the crisis arrived, the Government decided to refuse loans for schemes of conversion to oil. This refusal lasted from October/November 1956 to May 1957, when the crisis was deemed to be over. The restriction appears to have affected industrial users more lightly than non-industrial users. Nonetheless the switch from coal to oil was undoubtedly delayed, and the excessive output targets of the coal industry unnecessarily bolstered.

A footnote deserves to be written to all this. One Friday evening, after I had been toiling all day with the nuclear power programme, I was told by my private secretary that the official who had been negotiating with the political parties on their petrol ration had reached agreement with them. The agreement provided roughly for the same allocation as before, with an addition to take into account the increased political activity of post-war years. On the face of it this seemed reasonable enough and I accepted the arrangement.

The Sunday Express, however, in the person of Sir John Junor, interpreted the agreement as extending to members of Parliament. This was not in fact the case. Accordingly, in one of thoses silly pieces of theatre in which the House of Commons loves to revel, Sir John Junor was hauled before the bar of the House. He was clearly wrong in implying that the increase extended to members of Parliament. But he was right if he was implying that all the political parties had applied for, and had been granted, too much. Had I been less weary I might have noticed the fact; but I did not. I therefore owe to Sir John Junor a belated, though sincere, apology.

Meanwhile the sandstorm in the Middle East is blowing more ferociously than ever, while there are still no powers to introduce rationing. A retrospective judgement on the scheme introduced under my auspices would therefore point to the re-introduction in similar circumstances of roughly the same scheme. I hope only that it will not be necessary. A rationing scheme was prepared, but not put into force, after the increase in oil prices in 1973, but its nature is not known to me.

In the wake of the Suez crisis Sir Anthony Eden, alas, had to resign. This was a great sadness to me; subsequent life might have been different had he remained. He was succeeded as Prime Minister by Mr Harold Macmillan. I had been on a Saturday afternoon to watch a Chelsea football match. On my return home I found myself summoned to No. 10 Downing Street. I was told that I was going to be removed from Fuel and Power, that my successor would be an industrialist from the outside with a seat in the House of Lords, from which position he would be better placed to reconcile the Conservative Party to the fact of nationalisation. At home again I naturally telephoned my Permanent Secretary, Sir John (later Lord Redcliffe-) Maud. He came round later that evening and urged me to see the Prime Minister again. This I did on the Sunday morning.

I suggested that an attempt to reconcile the Conservative Party to nationalisation had to be done from the Commons, the Lords being too remote. I met with a stone wall. Mr Macmillan insisted that the House of Lords was the place from which the Conservative Party could be most effectively reconciled to nationalisation. The industrialist he ennobled was Sir Percy Mills – and I was the victim. My new office, it was indicated, might be the Ministry of Supply.

The controversy over nationalisation still goes on, 40 years after its initiation. What a way to run a country! But such is the fate of Ministers. They are birds of passage, arriving to pick up unpalatable morsels from predecessors, and leaving before they have accomplished what they hoped to achieve. I had hoped, for example, to revise the terms and conditions of appointment to nationalised boards. I had submitted proposals to this effect, including a provision that, on passage from the private to the public sector, the pension be made transferable. To this day no action has been taken on that particular provision. My only consolation on leaving the Ministry was a letter from my Permanent Secretary: 'I never expect to serve a Minister who did what you did – immediately giving us the sense you trusted us and wanted us to say what we thought, and at the same time the sense of authority and leadership.'

9

AN ENERGY POLICY

The myth runs that all the nationalised fuel and power industries are inefficient. The myth, fostered by the empty rhetoric of political parties, is almost entirely without foundation. Amidst the talk of 'privatisation' that requires saying; there is a case for nationalisation where private industry is unable or unwilling to do something which is economically desirable, or alternatively is unable to cope with the social aspects of its activity, for example, pollution or depletion. Judged by this criterion the nationalisation of all the fuel and power industries (oil excepted) was abundantly justified. The private coal industry was manifestly inefficient, under-investing and under-researching. The municipal or private gas and electricity undertakings were unable or unwilling so to sink their differences as to facilitate the formation of the national grid. They themselves thus made the case for nationalisation. The private firms invited to establish the nuclear power industry failed, in Lord Hinton's words, to contribute to the national prosperity. There was, however, no need to nationalise them, only to rationalise them.

Since nationalisation, the performance of the nationalised industries has varied, while apparently remaining unchanged over time. From the start electricity was over-ambitious, pitching its price low and attracting capital which could probably have been better invested elsewhere. This was Hugh Gaitskell's constant lament. The excess of ambition was extended at a later stage into the construction of conventional power stations, directed to an over-estimate of demand, and spilled over into the nuclear power programme. Coal likewise was over-ambitious from the very beginning, and remained so in spite of a failure to realise its ambitions. To this day it remains under-invested in new mines and over-invested in old mines. The performance of the gas industry is more difficult to assess, so rapid has been the change in its technology. There is no fundamental reason, however, to amend

63

the judgement that it has been efficient, though it is running into problems as North Sea gas reserves become depleted.

A broad view of the energy investment programme would probably run as follows: under-investment in new coal fields; continued over-investment in old coalfields; over-investment in conventional electrical power stations; under-investment in nuclear power, at any rate on economic grounds; adequate investment in gas, though the amount and nature of the investment may need to change as the sources of reserves change; and investment up to the limit in oil, though the rate of depletion has probably been too rapid. If this picture of energy investment is broadly right it has not been the result of a co-ordinated plan. It has stemmed from the haphazard decisions of individual industries and the mishaps which have sometimes befallen them. This is a far cry from the perfect harmony or the 'minimum of distortion' associated by ideologues with a 'perfect' market.

It is conventional to describe the three factors of production as land, capital and labour. New technology may be carrying us away from this conventional division. Fission through a fast reactor would require little in the way of land, though clearly much capital. Fusion would carry us farther still away from land, in that it would require no land for reprocessing. Energy therefore is on the point, if it is not already there, of becoming a factor of production on its own. To speak of it in terms of traditional markets is therefore a little old fashioned.

Chapter 3, as the starting chapter on fuel and power problems, opened with a statement by Mr Nigel Lawson, when Secretary of State for Energy: 'The Government's task is to set a framework which will ensure that the market operates in the energy sector with the minimum of distortion and that energy is produced and consumed efficiently.'

The subsequent chapters on each fuel and power source have suggested that practice is as follows. Coal is highly protected, with the result that its price in no way corresponds to a market price. The electricity industry has been forced to take a limited amount of coal and in the interests of coal, the exploitation of North Sea gas has been somewhat delayed. In the minds of the Department coal has reigned supreme, and to this extent the allocation of the energy market between different sources of energy has been 'distorted'.

In the case of both electricity and gas the price is primarily determined by the financial target fixed for the industry by the Government. If, to reach the financial target, the industry raises its prices and the market is not adversely affected, the industries' profits will rise and it is not irreverent to say that at a certain level of profits corporation tax can be extracted by the Inland Revenue. The primary determinant of price is thus the financial target, the response of the market playing a secondary role. It is to this extent and to this extent only that the market enters the picture.

Technology also enters into it. If sanction is given for the installation at Sizewell of a PWR and no undue delays affect subsequent PWRs, then the price of electricity should be lower than it otherwise would have been. The Government would presumably then adjust the industry's financial target. Would it raise it in the hope of higher profits from which corporation tax can be milked? Technology also enters into the pricing of gas. The synthesising of gas from coal is unlikely to be effected before the expiry of the gas reserves of the North Sea. With the exhaustion of supplies from the North Sea the price of gas is therefore likely to rise. Will the Government then raise the financial target too in the expectation that demand will not fall back and that profits will rise? Once again while the market will have played a part, the price will be an administered price.

The price of oil is now probably nearest to a market price, though only to the extent that the Organisation of Petroleum Exporting Countries (OPEC) producers can adapt their output to demand, an adaptation which is difficult while the world lolls in recession. As a country the United Kingdom is for the moment self-sufficient in oil, but having to export certain grades in order to obtain other grades. Production in the North Sea is probably at its peak – 2.5 million barrels a day (mbd). This is too small a quantity to affect the world price, which may therefore be said to be a market price.

The essential question is: are we primarily a fuel consuming country, ready to allow the consumer to choose his fuel at whatever price he cares to pay, or are we primarily a fuel producing country, concerned with regulating the rate of production and placing longer-term interests above the immediate interest of the consumer? Surely the facts suggest the latter. We are the only European country to possess hydro-carbons in all their amplitude – coal, oil and gas. Each supplies as follows to the total of our energy requirements: coal and oil about one-third each, natural gas about a quarter; and nuclear power a small fraction – 5 per cent. Other European countries have coal – e.g. Belgium – but not oil or gas. Yet other European countries still have oil and gas – e.g. Norway – but no coal. As a hydro-carbon producer we are unique in Europe, and our energy policy should therefore be that of a producer rather than that implied in Mr Lawson's statement – that of a country deferring to consumer wishes.

The Treasury has sought over the years to lay down guidelines for investment by nationalised industries. The broad purpose of these guidelines is to ensure that resources are not twisted or 'distorted' as between the public and private sectors. The concept of 'distortion' is an abstract one. It is based on the supposition that each producer is small, and pushes his production up to the point where the cost of any extra unit is equal to the price as established in the competitive market. In no industry is this concept more unreal than in the energy industry. The industrial units are large and there enter dimensions other than price – the security of supply and the vexing problem of pollution. As far as security of supply is concerned the richest area of oil is in the Middle East, the most highly explosive part of the political world. In the light of that fact what energy policy should we follow as a producer in place of our present non-existent policy? Surely, it should seek to promote cheapness of energy to British industry, particularly at a time when manufactured imports exceed manufactured exports and we are experiencing 'de-industrialisation', while at the same time ensuring long-term security (including safety) of supply.

The two criteria – cheapness to industry and long-term security – are not necessarily consonant with each other. We could rifle the North Sea now as we appear to be doing, and so supply industry with cheap oil, but without the long-term aim of safeguarding the resource, oil, which could yield revenue for future industrial investments, while at the same time safeguarding us from a possible eruption in the Middle East.

The two criteria can be reconciled only if we keep open all options. The policy towards North Sea oil should aim at long-term stability of output; after ascending to a peak, it could decline to a plateau – held there, if such a policy is open to the Government, as in the United States as new marginal fields are discovered to displace those exhausted.

If however, there were a conflagration in the Middle East we could scarcely keep our output entirely to ourselves. Other European countries would want their share. The policy towards Middle Eastern oil should be, in so far as it is within our power, to maintain the price and thus the ability of the countries concerned both to uphold and eventually, if need be, to expand production and industrial investment. In short, cheapness of supply to the British producer may not conduce to prosperity and peace in the Middle East.

The policy towards coal, should be to encourage imports, even if, at this stage, in small quantity, for an uprising in the Middle East or any resulting war could give rise to such a demand for coal that all near sources of imports could be closed to us. This might well mean importing coal at a price above the domestic price. There is indeed much misunderstanding over the comparative prices of imported and domestic coal. Coal extracted from near the surface in the western part of the United States could, at the point of extraction, be lower than the pithead price of coal in South Wales. To the initial cost, however, there would have to be added both the cost of transportation across the Atlantic and the cost within Britain of transport to the designated electrical power station. The total cost could conceivably be higher than the cost of extraction from an 'uneconomic' pit in South Wales. Even talk of an average cost of coal in the United Kingdom is unreal, for the real cost of extracting coal from a British pit has to be assessed in relation to the power station for which it is destined. It is this additional cost of transport to the power station which may render a pit 'economic' or 'uneconomic'.

It is not, however, coal which is likely to be in short supply. It is liquid fuels, used for certain chemical processes and for transportation. In the late 1970s over 60 per cent of the liquid fuels (oil and, to a much lesser extent, liquefied gas) went to the premium uses of chemicals and transport. In the United Kingdom over the last two decades two-thirds of the increase in the use of energy has been due to transport, and one-half due to private transport. Even though the increase in the use of energy as a whole may well decline in developed countries in relation to the Gross Domestic Product, the use of liquid fuels seems destined to increase. The possibility that by 2030 a yet higher proportion of all fuels will be required in liquid form is not too fanciful. Where are the liquids to be found? The conventional sources of oil will by then be near exhaustion. Resort would have to be had, at far higher cost and much capital expenditure, to unconventional sources of liquids, the shale of the Orinoco in Venezuela and the tar sands of Athabasca in Alberta. It is doubtful, however, whether, in combination, they would suffice for the foreseen need.

They would have to be complemented by another source – the gasification and liquefaction of coal. The technology is now known and it is not impossible to envisage production soon after the year 2000.

Naturally large investments would be required, the cost would be high, and ironically, many more miners would be needed. What is the young miner of 20, made redundant in 1985, to say in his forties as he reflects on a renewed drive for more miners?

The fossil fuels so far used – coal, oil and gas – are all polluting: that is, they emit carbon dioxide into the atmosphere. The resort to less conventional fossil fuels – shale, tar sands, liquefied coal – would result in even greater emission. The net outcome would be an increased emission of 'greenhouse' gases, of the order, of 1.5°C to 4.5°C, with the values in the lower part of the range being the more probable.[1]

An increase in global temperature of this magnitude would be without known precedent. The knowledge of the climate is so slight that the consequences can only be guessed – the western part of the United States made more arid, a retreat of the Arctic ice-cap, a rising level of the seas. This would be pollution on a grand scale, if by the word 'pollution' is meant a violent disturbance of the known environment.

Is there then some non-polluting source which we might seek? 'Market forces' would not help us for they know not of such intangibles: nor do they distinguish between the tenses, the future as against the present. Would the sun be a non-polluting source? Certainly it gives out energy. There are two possible ways in which this energy might be captured. Suppose a large number of mirrors were built in the Sahara, concentrating the sun's rays on a receiver, the concentrated heat of which in turn would give rise to steam and ultimately generate electrical power. The acreage to be covered would be vast, the apparatus complicated and costly, and the electrical power, when produced, would need to be distributed to the northern hemisphere, over multiple frontiers. This is certainly no easy task. And the same can be said of an assemblage of photovoltaic cells. The sun then provides no early answer.

Nor does water, though clean enough in itself. The amount of hydro-electric power in the world at large could possibly be doubled, though not in the United Kingdom. But no one can foretell the effect on the riverine vegetation. Finally, there is the wind, dispersed and fitful. It might, however, be captured by the clusters of windmills way out to sea, thus causing some disfigurement of the maritime scene.

[1]   *Changing Climate*, National Academy Press, Washington DC, 1983, p. 2.

Energy from the sun, from water or from wind would require a much larger use of land than nuclear power and this would be a form of pollution.

We are then condemned to carry on as long as we can with our present polluting forms of energy, or else find an alternative. The only alternative is nuclear power. Nuclear fission does not emit gases into the atmosphere; but it leaves behind it radioactive waste which, unless firmly sealed, is contaminating. Nuclear fusion would emit virtually no gases, and the amount of radioactive waste may be less than that from fission. Fusion, however, is according to some, at least a century away, though others would contend that it would be practicable earlier.

The choice then is not between one form of energy which is clean and another which is unclean. The choice is between different forms of uncleanliness.

For my own part I opt for nuclear power, believing that it can be safely contained. The decision, however, will not be mine; it will be that of the great British public, which as yet is unenlightened on the issues.

If the answer is indeed nuclear power, the question arises what form of reactor? The era of what might be called the 'conventional' reactors – PWR, AGR, etc. – will be relatively short, although they could still be in operation in the second half of the next century. The long-term future would appear to belong to the breeder or fast reactors, for the simple reason that 'about 60 times more energy could be extracted from a given amount of uranium than if it were used in thermal reactors'[2]; 'the national stockpile of 20,000 tonnes of depleted uranium provides us with an indigenous energy source equal to the estimated economically recoverable coal resources in the United Kingdom, and sufficient to meet electricity demand at current levels for some 400 years even without taking into account any other source of electricity'.[3] By the time that existing power stations – that is, those in operation and under construction are closed down, they will have left behind a stockpile of the isotope U238 sufficient to guarantee electricity supply for a thousand years and would be entirely indigenous to the United Kingdom. There appears to be no answer to that.

The history has shown that electricity and gas became integrated

[2]   Sir Peter Hirsch, Sir John Cockcroft Memorial Lecture, 15 September 1983.
[3]   Ibid.

systems as a result of nationalisation, the previous individual undertakings having proved incapable of integrating themselves. An integrated system is of particular importance in the case of nuclear power, for it provides, among other things, a single centre to carry responsibility for all safety aspects, a powerful centre for research and development, and a very small number of customers to confront the now single plant supplier, the National Nuclear Corporation.

The energy policy outlined is a policy related to production. Within the constraints of a national policy aimed at keeping open all production possibilities, the consumer is free to choose. His freedom is, however, extremely limited, the main determinants of the constraints being the national authorities. The policy of keeping open all production options has already been weakened to some degree by the policy of 'privatisation'; we are no longer potential masters of North Sea oil, except in so far as we choose to lay down production levels for the private oil companies, and of that there is no sign. 'Privatisation' of electricity and gas would reduce the benefits to be derived from scale and in particular weaken the ability to undertake research and development. Neither of these consequences would be of any benefit to the consumer. Neither therefore conforms with the criteria laid down in this chapter for energy policy in a situation of great uncertainty – cheapness to British industry so long as this is consistent with long-term security (including safety) of supply, and the least possible pollution.

10

AIRCRAFT

At the close of Mr Macmillan's period as Chancellor of the Exchequer – the end of 1956 – the economic situation was no better than it had been a year previously. The drain on the gold and dollar reserves was worse. Borrowing from abroad could have been resorted to, but it had to be reinforced by internal restraint. This restraint was all the more necessary since the oil shortage would cause production to rise by less than incomes and consumer demand, with the risk of a stronger inflationary pressure. I therefore proposed an increase of between 3 and 5 pence a gallon in the price of oil products. How far the worsened situation was due to the policy of cuts and therefore the reduced investment and the reduced income which might have been derived from it, and how far due to the Suez crisis is an open question. Whatever the respective contributions the answer from on high was again 'cuts'. This time the 'cuts' bore most heavily, at least as far as I, as Minister of Supply, was concerned, on defence, and cuts in defence should in theory have a beneficial effect on exports and investments.

Early in 1957, soon after his inception as Prime Minister, Mr Macmillan issued a directive which made the Minister of Defence the sole determinant of the defence programme, subject presumably to Cabinet agreement. Previously the Minister of Defence consulted with the Service Ministers before drawing up his defence plan. Now he was apparently his own master. This was the first step on the road towards a unification of the defence structure, of which more was to be heard later.

I should have guessed this when I was offered the Ministry of Supply. I demurred, knowing that my predecessor, the late Reginald Maudling, had recommended the disappearance of the Ministry. When I mentioned this, the Prime Minister said emphatically, 'No'. Pointing theatrically across to the Admiralty, he said: 'There are the villains', by which word, I take it, he embraced the entirety of the armed forces. His intention, he said was to create a powerful Ministry of Defence and a powerful Ministry of Materiel, myself in the latter role. Accordingly, I accepted, little realising how, in the new capacity, I was to be dragged behind the grinding wheels of Mr Sandys' chariot, Mr (later Lord) Sandys being the new Minister of Defence.

My first task as Minister of Supply was to reply to a letter sent to me by Mr Peter (now Lord) Thorneycroft, the new Chancellor of the Exchequer, requesting me to cancel the Olympus engine. My predecessor (Reggie Maudling) had, he said, agreed to cancellation; and the advice of my Permanent Secretary was certainly to cave in. I asked to see the file. The more I read it, the more convinced I became that the Olympus should not be cancelled. I replied accordingly to the Chancellor, making the case as cogent as I could. The Chancellor never answered and the Olympus continued, being, in a developed form, the engine which ultimately powered the Concorde, and could have powered the ill-fated TSR2.

Mr Sandys' defence policy rested on two apparently simple pillars: an 'independent element' (whatever that might mean) of the nuclear deterrent in the shape of a land-based ballistic missile; and the substitution of missiles for aircraft for the air defence of these islands. As far as I recollect, the only Minister to support my own protest that the policy would weaken our ability to fight a conventional war was Lord Hailsham. It has been said that Mr Sandys' interest in missiles derived from the study of the German V2 rockets which Churchill had asked him to undertake towards the close of the war. The rationale put forward for his twin policy was the need to relieve the strain imposed on the national economy by the level of defence spending. In other words a nuclear force was supposedly cheaper than a conventional force.

The policy had far-reaching implications. It meant, for one thing, a weakening of our ability to hold east of Suez by conventional means. It also meant a reduction in our naval forces, though it was questioned whether this would warrant the transfer of certain naval commands to other countries. National service would be brought to an end, and while certain Nato countries might object, it was for us (it was contended) to decided on the nature of our contribution to Nato, and not our Nato allies. Finally and most importantly, the Chiefs of Staff emphasised that the reduction in total forces from 410,000 to 375,000 could not be justified on strictly military grounds, but was dictated primarily by economic needs. Responsibility for the changed policy therefore lay solely on political shoulders.

For example, the politicians grossly underestimated the cost of the ballistic missile, which went by the name of Blue Streak. Its history was chequered. The Air Ministry had begun to express an interest way back in 1954, realising that manned bombers would be obsolete in the 1960s. In the same year the United States Administration, bound by the McMahon Act of 1946 not to reveal any information on the nuclear warhead, proposed a joint programme – they would help us, that is, with information on the delivery vehicle. The joint programme went ahead in 1955, at an estimated cost over ten years of £50 million.

The missile's range was a maximum 1,200 miles, inadequate for a deterrent. Hence possibly the subsequent huffing and puffing. Before 1957 was out Mr Sandys, having previously acclaimed the weapon, had ordered a slowing down. In the following year he was all for acceleration. Mr Selwyn Lloyd, the Secretary of State for Foreign Affairs, was the only one to express concern over the public reaction to nuclear weapons. But the conclusion which he drew from his own concern was an acceleration of tests. The tests were carried out on Christmas Island, in the Pacific, and, on a smaller scale, at Maralinga, in the parched but beautiful Australian desert, north-west of Adelaide. On the morrow of one such test at Maralinga, a family of trekking Aborigines were found ensconced in the hole made by the atomic explosion. After decontamination they were sent on to the next station, which was instructed to supply them with another dingo in substitution for their own, which had had to be destroyed. From a different point of view (the financial), Mr Thorneycroft wanted a re-examination of the case for a marine-based missile. Such a re-examination meant a further slowing-down. And every slowing-down added to the eventual cost.

The contractor – de Havilland – did not help. The financial control was lax. Before the decade of the 1950s was out the cost had risen to over £300 million – six times the original estimate. Finally, in 1960 the weapon was cancelled, the resulting saving to the defence budget being over £400 million. It is ironical now to reflect that both the Lord President (Lord Salisbury) and the Minister of Defence were keen on space research – that is, the putting of instruments into space with a rocket, which could be either American or Blue Streak. The Minister of Defence was of the view that if we were to maintain our position as a leading scientific country we should adapt Blue Streak. Alas, Blue

Streak was already losing out in its main role as a military weapon. No one was interested in a subsidiary role. And the role of launching satellites into space has passed to France.

The cost of Blue Streak, a weapon mistakenly chosen to save costs, did not, however, end there. The Air Ministry could not be expected to give up lightly and forever the idea of the manned aircraft. The white paper of 1957, which virtually abolished all aircraft, had therefore to be circumvented. The vehicle chosen for circumvention was the TSR (Tactical, Strike, Reconnaisance) 2. It was in effect an all-purpose aircraft: it could fly low; it could fly high; it could deliver tactical bombs to support advancing forces; and it could deliver a strategic bomb – that is, a bomb at long distance to destroy, if need be, cities. The Air Ministry invited me to intercede with the Minister of Defence to obtain his support for the aircraft; I refused. The specification was drawn up with the help of the late Sir Frederick Brundrett, Chief Scientist to the Ministry of Defence. Consent from the Ministry of Defence having been obtained, partly presumably on his advice, an announcement was made in the 1959 White Paper on Defence.

The paper life of the aircraft, however, scarcely lasted half a decade, such was the speed at which the costs mounted. At the moment of approval the estimated cost was around £75 million. By the advent of the Labour Government in the autumn of 1964 the cost must have been hovering around £300 million. Why such an increase? The main contractor for the airframe was Vickers, which had never been noted for keeping costs down. The Ministry of Supply (later Aviation) had, however, direct contact with the engine manufacturer – Bristol – and the electronics firm – Ferranti. Had Vickers been well enough equipped, it should have been entrusted with a turnkey contract, with responsibility for both engine and electronic costs. Vickers, however, were only in part to blame.

The chief culprit was the aircraft itself. An aircraft for all things was of such complexity that it was bound to be subject to frequent changes of design, each change adding to the costs. The main lesson of the TSR2 was that the development and manufacture in this country of small numbers of a complex aircraft – 50 were envisaged – did not make sense. It was not therefore surprising that under the Labour Government of 1964–70 the TSR2 was cancelled, the American aircraft TFX (later re-baptised the F111) being purchased in its place. The total cost of the purchase was roughly equal to the cost of the further development of the TSR2 plus the cost of a substantial purchase of the F111. Three prototypes of the TSR2 were built, but they seem to have remained in their sheds, never flown.

In between Blue Streak and the TSR2 there appeared an interloper – Thunderbolt – an American missile, launched from the air, like the present-day Cruise, and to be adopted by ourselves. For some reason the Americans decided to cancel it, but without consultation with ourselves. A British visitor to Washington learned by accident of the cancellation. Alive to the furore which the fact would provoke in this country, he alerted the then Ambassador, Lord Harlech. 'I do wish', Lord Harlech said, 'that they would convey this kind of information officially.'

Thus a defence programme which had set out to cut defence spending had resulted in two projects – Blue Streak and the TSR2 – which were not only abortive, but which had also cost immense sums. How large those sums were in relation to what might otherwise have been the case is a hypothetical question which no one can now answer. The substitution for the TSR2 of the US F111 – the precursor of Cruise – had been rendered possible by the abolition of the McMahon Act in 1958. Whether the abolition of the McMahon Act had been due to our own simplistic effort to develop a deterrent weapon I cannot say. All I know is that, early in 1957, Mr Quarles, Under-Secretary of State and at that stage ranking ahead of the Secretaries of the Army, the Navy and the Air Force, at the Pentagon, had said to me that the United States Administration would have been disquieted if the United Kingdom were not seen to be 'pulling her weight' in deterrent weapons.

The lesson of the TSR2 – namely, that the United Kingdom market was too small for a number of manufacturing firms and a handful of customers – was a long time a-learning. In vain did I try to impress upon the aircraft constructors – still flushed with war-time triumph – that they needed to coalesce into units of greater strength and form links with emerging units on the European Continent. In their view nobody on the Continent was worthwhile talking to – but they were looking behind and not ahead. As for the customers, there were then only three – BEA, BOAC and Transport Command of the RAF. The aircraft industry needed them to draw their specification for purposes beyond the United Kingdom and to place their orders with constructors of financial strength. The airlines preferred – and possibly still prefer – to remain independent and therefore insular.

The first tussle arose over the Trident, an aircraft desired by BEA.

There were two competitors – Hawker Siddeley, who proclaimed themselves ready to undertake the project as a private venture, that is at their own cost, and de Havilland, a weaker firm financially and desirous of financial support from the Ministry of Supply. BEA were firm in their preference for the de Havilland offer. I opposed the preference, partly because it entailed expenditure for development from my Department, partly because I considered the specification not to be applicable world-wide. In the light of the offer by Hawker Siddeley to build the project with their own finances, de Havilland amended their offer to make it a private venture too. I considered the offer specious (the sequel was to vindicate the judgement), but in so far as it was made no further cost was threatened to my Department. There was, however, a cost to the Government – an investment by BEA had to be approved. Though my Department was now less directly involved, I still considered the specification to be unique to BEA and so remained opposed to the investment. Nonetheless the project went ahead. The result is now known – the specification was indeed out of accord with world requirements and, as a result, the project was a commercial failure. It thus flew the same flight path as the Comet, the Vanguard and the VC10.

So concerned was I over the plight of the aircraft industry – our second largest exporter of engineering products – that towards mid-1957 I put the problem to the Cabinet. I pointed out that the cost of research even of civil aircraft had hitherto been borne in the main on the defence budget, and that aero-engines similarly had been first tried out on military aircraft. 'Unless', I said, 'the opportunity is taken to bring home to the nationalised corporations the need for partnership with the Government, I am afraid I see little future for the civil aircraft industry in this country.' I suggested therefore that the Government should use such power of procurement as remained to it to shape the industry into units which were fewer in numbers but financially stronger. Similarly the Government should seek to harmonise the requirements of the airline corporations and of Transport Command so as to ensure that the initial domestic order for an aircraft should be as large as possible. At the same time I indicated that the resources released as a result of the defence cuts should be readily absorbed by the civil economy, but that the contraction in defence research and development was likely to entail a net reduction in national investment in scientific facilities. The Prime Minister agreed that the problem was serious and remitted it to a committee under the chairmanship of the Chancellor of the Exchequer.

The Chancellor, now Mr Heathcot (late Lord) Amory, reported little less than a year later. It was agreed that the aircraft industry was of sufficient importance to warrant a higher level of financial support than that accorded to other industries. The industry should, however, be pressed to assume a progressively larger share of the costs of development if the country were to avoid the charge of subsidising exports. This was possible only if the industry formed itself into financially stronger units. The policy which I had put forward had thus, at least in part, been endorsed. A statement was drawn up by officials for me to make in the House of Commons. The wording was not of the happiest, and I suggested one or two small changes. I was told that if one comma were changed, the entire issue would have to be re-opened, so many Departments having now agreed to it. And so in the Commons, I mouthed my policy in words not of my composition.

The layman may well ask whether all this to-do was really necessary. I do not believe it was. The Cabinet could quite easily have agreed to my original submission, subject to agreement with the Chancellor on costs in specific cases. But government somehow seems to like to march in serried ranks, Ministers and officials deliberating over several months in galactic unison, to enunciate a conclusion which had been obvious from the beginning.

It was not long before the unison was put to the test. It so happened that two firms put forward projects of identical specification – Hawker Siddeley with the Avro 748 and Handley Page with the Herald. Hawker Siddeley had a degree of financial strength; Handley Page, on the other hand, was financially weak. No British customer wanted either aircraft, though BEA were ready, if need be, to carry out proving trials of the Herald. I considered that neither aircraft justified financial support from the Government, the design containing nothing technologically advanced. Lord Mills, on the other hand, who had been given an arbitrating function between myself, as the sponsor of the aircraft industry, and the Minister of Transport, as the sponsor of the airlines, a function to which I did not object, took a different view. In his capacity as chairman of the Cabinet sub-committee on civil aviation, he contended that the Government should give financial support to the Herald. Such support, he maintained, represented an extension of existing policy rather than a departure from it.

The divergence between us was complete. There was no alternative but to take the issue to the Cabinet. I was prepared to compromise to the extent that if the Government wanted to give financial support that support should be to the Avro 748 rather than to the Herald. I based my case on two grounds: first, Hawker Siddeley was financially the stronger company; secondly, I was reasonably certain that the Indian Government would place an order for the construction of 200 of the Avro 748 aircraft at Bangalore.

I had been to India in the spring of 1959. Commenting on my visit Malcolm Macdonald, the High Commissioner, wrote:

> we were all struck by ... the friendly ease and intimacy of the relationship which he [Mr A. J.] has established with Mr Krishna Menon, who is often far from genial to deal with. In my opinion the friendship between Mr A. J. and Mr Menon is of value to the U.K. far beyond the departmental interests of the Ministry of Supply. Mr Menon is a Minister with widespread influence in shaping the present Indian Government's policies, and it is not impossible that his significance will grow rather than diminish in years to come.

I doubt whether any member of the Cabinet had read this dispatch.

At the Cabinet meeting the Prime Minister agreed that the proposal to support the Herald was a reversal of the general policy agreed upon. Nonetheless he supported his confidant – I suppose he could scarcely do anything else. Lord Mills opined that there was a market in the world for 1500 of the relevant type of aircraft. Since the Government had no market research unit, the figure must have been derived from Handley Page or plucked out of the air. Once again, the future market was grossly exaggerated. Going round the table, starting with Iain Macleod on my left, the Prime Minister obtained support from everybody, with two exceptions, Reggie Maudling and Heathcot Amory. I was defeated and in the House of Commons I defended a decision which I knew to be indefensible.

But the story was not yet over. From Delhi the High Commissioner reported that the decision had placed the Indian order for the Avro 748 in jeopardy, without any likelihood of an Indian order for the Herald. The Prime Minister accordingly took it upon himself to reverse the Cabinet's decision, telegraphing the Indian Prime Minister in June 1959 that the British Government would give financial support to the Avro 748 unconditionally. In the event the Indians placed their order as I had predicted, the Avro 748 was sold in some hundreds, and as a result of the effort to continue with the Herald, Handley Page was forced into liquidation. As part of the sequel de Havilland requested financial aid for the Trident, a request which I assume was granted. It is clear that the Prime Minister and Lord Mills were working hand in hand. But what were they after? The only logical answer is that Mr Harold Macmillan had belatedly recognised that the policy of 'cuts' had gone too far and that he had now to go into reverse thrust. Instead of 'cuts' the cry was now 'spend, spend, spend'. On the morrow of my return from India I found that the Parliamentary Secretary had summoned a meeting of officials to discuss the injunction to spend more 'without', of course, 'incurring inflation'. Just as under the policy of 'cuts' the Treasury's preoccupation had been with the management of the Government debt to the neglect of the efficiency of the nationalised industries, so now under the policy of 'spend' industrial structure became of secondary priority. Whatever the macroeconomic policy, industrial structure was always the Cinderella.

I had a final example of this. Because of the commercial failure both of the Vanguard and the VC10 Vickers were in serious financial difficulties. My aid was sought, to the total tune of £21 million. Before approaching a decision I invited Mr Henry (now Lord) Benson, a senior partner of Coopers and Lybrand to look for me into the affairs of the company. He reported that the prospective loss on the VC10 was £15 million and that the losses were due to a gross under-estimate of costs. He recommended that Government help should not exceed £12 million, that the levy normally receivable by the Government in return for financial aid should be waived for all VC10s sold over and above the 35 bought by BOAC and that the assistance should be *preceded* by a scheme of rationalisation. I put these recommendations to the Cabinet, specifying that the act of rationalisation should be an amalgamation of Vickers with English Electric and, if possible, de Havilland.

It so happened that Mr Benson was invited to attend a meeting of the Vickers board. There he learned of the board's certainty that the Cabinet would not accept my proposal for rationalisation. There could be only one cause for the certainty – the knowledge that Lord Mills would not go along with me. Never nominally appointed an overlord, Lord Mills acted the overlord, covertly and indiscreetly.

Even before this incident I had written to the Prime Minister complaining that the identity of members of the Cabinet sub-committee on civil aviation was known to the industry. Every member therefore, was potentially a victim of lobbying. That is the kernel of the case for keeping secret the identity of members of Cabinet sub-committees, particularly if they are concerned with the disbursement of monies.

The aircraft industry had not presented a pretty picture – ignorance of markets, laxity of costs, and greed for public money. I had tried to cope with the problem through rationalisation. In the end I had been thwarted. As I later put it in my lone note of dissent from the recommendations of the Plowden Committee,[1] which had proposed a degree of Government ownership of the industry:

> Soon after the middle fifties the industry was ready to embark on a number of civil projects wholly financed by itself. By the end of the decade it was seeking Government help and obtained it. If the Government were now to purchase part of the equity it would again be appearing as a rescuer . . . and another rescue would be an inauspicious start to what should be a new attempt to inculcate into the industry a sense of financial discipline . . . a policy for the industry should in my view attempt, not to build on weakness, but to reinforce the points of strength.

Even an amalgamation of British firms, however, was not enough. Links had to be established with constructors in other countries. An opportunity arose when I received a report from the technicians recommending a start on a supersonic civil aircraft. In the 1950s we had dominated Europe with the Viscount; in the 1960s we had been ousted by the French Caravelle; might we in the 1970s re-establish a position in common with the French? I was prompted in this view by our refusal to have anything to do with the European Community, a refusal which I considered mistaken.

Accordingly in June 1959 I went to Paris and proposed to the French Government that we study together the possibility of building jointly a supersonic civil aircraft. I was warmly received, and a committee was set up comprising three experts from each side. When I reported back to London that technical collaboration with the French was possible, the Cabinet, consistently with their scorn for Europe, laughed with derision. Nonetheless I was allowed £250,000–£300,000 to conduct a feasibility study. Thus was Concorde born.

The midwife later was, of course, Lord Mills, and whether at that stage I would wish to have acknowledged fatherhood I do not know. Whether because of Concorde or not the industry had overcome its

[1] Report of the Committee of Inquiry into the Aircraft Industry, 1965, Cmnd. 2853.

insularity. Technically, the Airbus, constructed by a loose consortium of firms in this country, France and Germany, with France inevitably in the lead, was a success; whether it was so commercially I do not know. If this international co-operation stemmed from Concorde – and it did certainly not precede it – then Concorde had a spin-off which does not feature in the narrower figures ascribed to that project.

International co-operation should not, however, stop at Europe. It should also extend to the United States. The Plowden Committee was sceptical of this possibility. I was more hopeful. And events proved me right. The classic example of such Anglo-American co-operation was the Harrier. The concept was Hawker Siddeley's. The company, however, had the sense to realise that it lacked the resources for development. Accordingly development was entrusted to the American firm, MacDonnell Douglas. That is how it should be.

Since my concern had been with aircraft constructors I had thought of internationalisation only in respect of them. Equally important, however, was the internationalisation of the buyers, who lay outside my purview. Enough has been said of the uniqueness of specification demanded by the British airline. Internationalisation of specification for military aircraft was not too difficult to contrive, since Western European countries are members of Nato. Civil aircraft, however, are a different matter. As far as I know, no attempt had been made to promote the amalgamation of European airlines. Yet this is what an imaginative view of the European Economic Community would have tried to achieve.

Worse, British Airways are to be 'privatised'. Even when publicly owned they paid little regard to the needs of the British aircraft industry. When they are 'privatised' the Government will have lost all influence over procurement policy for civil aircraft, and procurement is one of the most important tools available to a government to promote technology. It would be ironical if the 'privatisation' of British Airways had an adverse effect on the prospects of British Aerospace, the now 'privatised' consortium of British aircraft constructors. Aerospace has at the moment plenty of military orders, although these are always subject to uncertainty; it has little in the way of civil work; the 'privatisation' of British Airways is scarcely likely to increase that little.

In summary the British aircraft industry contributed to the British economic decline by an over-long attachment to the memory of an embattled but victorious Britain. Too late did it perceive the resurgence of others. Now it is one with them – perhaps a little behind them, with its position likely to be further weakened by the 'privatisation' of British Airways. In mitigation of the weakness of the aircraft industry it should be said that it was probably the victim of an ideology – namely, that competition is always better than non-competition. The truth of the proposition depends entirely on the size of the geographical unit. In the case of the aircraft and the airline industries, technology has outgrown the scale of the administrative unit, just as it had in earlier days in gas and electricity. The administrative unit had now to be international in scale. Few people, however, were or are ready so to broaden their outlook beyond what they had been taught in youth.

In between the saga of the aircraft industry there was sandwiched a further development in the structure of defence. Without much, if any, warning there was sprung upon the Cabinet a white paper creating the new post of Chief of Defence Staff in place of that of the chairman of the Chiefs of Staff Committee; the new Chief of Defence Staff was also to act as Chief of Staff to the Ministry of Defence. No longer was there any talk of a great Ministry of Materiel; with the Service Ministers I was to be a satrap of the emperor at Defence. The main purpose of the white paper was to confirm on a 'permanent' basis the arrangements which had been introduced provisionally when Mr Macmillan became Prime Minister at the beginning of 1957.

The word 'permanent' was, however, a piece of legerdemain. There were two opposing views: the traditional, according to which the Minister of Defence consulted with Service Ministers; and the newer view that the Minister of Defence should be empowered to override Service Ministers without reference to a higher authority. This latter view would have required legislation, though why this was put off I did not really understand. The white paper was a compromise, liable therefore to different interpretations. It was defeated, primarily by Lord Hailsham, mainly, I suspect, on the ground of the unexpectedness with which it had been thrust before the Cabinet. The Prime Minister retreated before Hailsham's fury and a new draft was submitted, the main feature of which was that it removed any ground for suspecting that the Chief of Defence Staff might seek advice from the Services without the knowledge of the Chief of Staff concerned. I doubted myself whether this amendment warranted the withdrawal of the earlier white paper. Either the white paper should have been withdrawn in its entirety, because of the misunderstandings implicit in its 'compromise', or the Prime Minister should have gone the 'whole hog' and legislated. Security was another subject which occasionally crossed my ken. Hinton has written in his memoirs: 'I am sure that MI5, the organisation concerned with counter-espionage in this country, ran a tight security service but I had always felt that they achieved their results by meticulous attention to detail rather than by the exercise of a noticeably high level of intelligence.' I felt very much the same. Twice I felt the long arm of MI5 stretching mysteriously from behind. The first occasion was at the Ministry of Fuel and Power, where the Permanent Secretary informed me that an able official had to be denied promotion because his wife was allegedly a communist. He is now the chairman of an important company and is probably in possession of far more real secrets than he had at the Ministry of Fuel and Power. The second occasion was at the Ministry of Supply, where a scientist, having conceived an admiration for Soviet technology, had taken to reading the communist daily newspaper, *The Morning Star*; it was recommended to me that he be removed from all classified (i.e. highly secret) work. I, too, at the Ministry of Fuel and Power, had been a regular reader of *The Morning Star*. On both occasions I deferred, not because I thought either case was just, but because of the possibility that had anything gone wrong, I, the Minister, would have been held responsible. Leaks there were a-plenty; invariably attempts were made to track them down and invariably they failed. But nobody really cared; the leaks, while embarrassing, were never considered to be of importance.

Finally, I was preoccupied with the Royal Ordnance Factories, of which I had inherited 23. They were no longer needed for war in that number, but were equally not equipped or organised for civil production. There was no alternative therefore to a reduction in numbers. The essential question, still unanswered, was: How many should be retained in public hands? The fundamental reason for keeping some in public ownership is that they carry a reserve of capacity ready for use in case of military emergency. If all are 'privatised' it is difficult to see how any reserve capacity can be kept in being without a subsidy.

My time at the Ministry of Supply was over. After the General Election of 1959 Mr Macmillan offered me the Ministry of Works, an offer which I had no hesitation in turning down. I did not believe that the Prime Minister's confidant was capable of not interfering in whatever was proceeding industrially, even remotely, and I certainly had no faith in his judgement; accordingly I retired to the back benches.

For the economist the main question posed by the period 1955–9 is this: was the exaggerated retrenchment followed by an equally exaggerated expansion, of which the Handley Page Herald was a minor sympton, a reflection merely of Mr Macmillan's character or did it lie in the nature of things? I tend to the view that it lay in the nature of things. The Government's main control is over capital investment. This is slow to contract and after a contraction, slow to expand. And the sluggishness in turn makes Ministers impatient; they then over-do things, and so the management of demand by 'fine tuning' becomes almost an impossibility.

11
TECHNOLOGY

Apart from aircraft, the preoccupying concern of the Ministry of Supply was technology. As the aircraft programme dwindled, there arose the prospect of redundant scientific teams. What was one to do with them? To allow their dispersal in fragments to other parts of British industry with little knowledge of their tradition or potential? Or to hold them as teams while feeding them with non-aircraft or at any rate non-military projects? My instinct inclined to the latter course.

Towards the end of 1957 I sent to Mr Macmillan a paper[1] suggesting the transformation of the Ministry of Supply into a Ministry of Technology. My concern with technology was based on a perception that it was an important key to economic growth. For example, 'From one third to one half of all the growth in the American economy to the present (i.e. roughly 100 years) has come from technological change.'[2] The purpose of my memorandum was two-fold: to facilitate the transfer of knowledge from the military to the civil field; and to utilise the expertise developed in the placing of military research and development contracts to put it also at the disposal of civil industry.

This knotty problem was remitted to Sir Norman (later Lord Norman-Brook) Brook, as secretary to the Cabinet. He chaired innumerable meetings of Permanent Secretaries to consider my paper. Each Permanent Secretary had a vested interest. Either he was the head of a military Department, and fearful therefore that the proposal would weaken the military research effort; or he was the head of a civil Department, anxious lest the bias of the proposed new Ministry be overwhelmingly military. The answer was a lemon. If ever there was a case for an independent 'think-tank', giving objective advice to

---

[1] Appendix 1.
[2] Ralph Landaü *Technology, Economics and Policies*, National Academy of Engineering, Washington, DC, 1982.

the entire Cabinet this was it. A conclave of Departmental custodians was no substitute.

In the event, Mr Macmillan went into the 1959 election proclaiming the formation of a new Ministry of Science. There was much dispute over the preposition 'for' or 'of'. 'Of' implied to some a dictation by the Minister: 'for', by contrast implied that he was a servant of science. The Minister, it later transpired, was to be Lord Hailsham. This was the very reverse of what I had in mind. I was after the speedier passage of knowledge (science) into the doing of things (technology). The result was to make even worse the unevenness of the British scientific –technological spectrum – the balance was tilted even further against technology. In the course of the press conference held on his appointment Lord Hailsham made two interesting comments – one illustrative of himself, the other of a more permanent nature. He could not, he said, see himself enthusing over any scientific project. When later an attempt was made to make him an Honorary Doctor of Science at Cambridge University, the scientific community of the university rose in revolt. More importantly the British parliamentary system required, he said, that Ministers be amateurs, advised by experts. That is not quite true, the advisers, more often than not, being 'generalists' rather than experts. It was against the 'generalist' tradition that Lord Fulton railed some ten years later in his Report on the British Civil Service.[3]

The debate between 'generalists' and experts is in my view misconceived. The British educational system is such that we are nearly all brought up as specialists. Outside our specialist field we are amateurs. Nonetheless a Minister in charge of a scientific/technological Department who has some knowledge of science is better able to grasp the whole than his counterpart who has specialised in the humanities. Certainly I consider I should have been a better Minister of Supply had I possessed a modicum of scientific knowledge.

With the passage of time a Ministry of Technology came into being. I was friendly with the late Patrick Blackett, who had some influence over Harold Wilson. With the formation of the Wilson Government of 1964 there was created a Ministry of Technology, deliberately, on Patrick Blackett's advice, kept apart from the Ministry of Supply, now expanded to Aviation, so as to include the airlines. The first Minister of Technology was Mr Frank Cousins, who kept the Department small.

[3]   Report on the Civil Service, Cmnd. 3638, 1984.

It concerned itself with four main industries – computers, electronics, instruments and machine tools. All four industries had a common feature – they exported at low cost to developing countries and imported at higher cost from industrialised countries. In other words, we were exporting less sophisticated products and importing more sophisticated ones. This point has since been expanded by Professor Brian Reddaway.

> The UK has shown a tendency to lose out to the more progressive developed countries on advanced products, such as electronic goods (Japan) or large passenger aeroplanes (USA), through slowness in product development and/or inferior marketing; it also tends to lose out to the newly industrialising countries on such things as bulk textiles because of their lower wages. This largely explains the persistent growth of import penetration in the UK markets for manufactured goods – though reduction of trade barriers has also helped.[4]

This tendency became greatly aggravated during Mrs Thatcher's regime. '. . . in the first quarter of 1983 the volume of imported manufacturers was 19 per cent above the 1979 level, whilst UK output of manufactures was 15 per cent down and UK exports down by 5 per cent.'[5]

Mr Cousins was succeeded by Mr Anthony Wedgewood Benn, who, while greatly expanding the Department, seemed to think primarily in terms of social experiment, for example, the transformation into workers' co-operatives of companies which had little chance of success, and of regional aid. Regional aid may give a firm an initial fillip; but it is an uncertain prop, for later it may be withdrawn. Mr Benn does not appear to have given the Ministry a technological impulse.

But perhaps it is unfair to blame the Ministry of Technology; it is the system which was to blame. What was technology for? What was its over-riding aim? Was it to reverse the trend of low value exports and high value imports? If so, the policy was not made explicit. Now that the Ministry of Technology has changed (declined?) into a Department of Industry there is still no declared policy.

The absence of objective is epitomised in the following statement: 'total Government spending on Research and Development is not determined centrally and then distributed among possible ben-

4   W. B. Reddaway, 'Problems and Prospects for the UK Economy', *Economic Record*, September 1983, p. 225.   5   Ibid.

eficiaries: it is the aggregate of a number of separate department decisions.'[6] In other words, there is no sense of priorities.

The British organisation for science and technology may broadly be described as follows. Floating on high is the Advisory Council for Applied Research and Development (ACARD). As the name indicates, ACARD's function is to advise; there is no executive power. Seldom in fact has the Government sought ACARD's advice and the subjects reported on have been chosen almost exclusively by ACARD itself. The reports receive a formal response from the Secretary of State for Industry, a response with which ACARD has invariably disagreed. The reports appear to be so many arrows shot into the air haphazardly; eventually they may hit a mark, but the hitting seems to take a long time. The impression left on the relevant House of Lords Committee, as expressed by Lord Flowers, was one of 'massive inaction on the part of the whole Government machine in spite of splendid efforts on the part of ACARD . . . to shift things along'.[7]

Beneath ACARD there sit the array of Requirements Boards in different Ministries, primarily in the Department of Industry. The Boards place contracts either with a Government research laboratory or with a private undertaking in accordance with what are considered to be the needs of the customer. The philosophy guiding the placing of contracts was expressed by Sir Peter Carey, former Permanent Secretary to the Department of Industry:

> In our work . . . we are trying all the time to get as close as possible to the market through our requirements board system where we have on those boards eminent industrialists who themselves are working in the market place and understand the needs of the market better than civil servants who are sitting in Whitehall and may be insulated from these influences.[8]

Is the market necessarily right? Contrast Sir Peter's view with the German view: 'the market temporarily underrates better technological solutions because supply and demand are governed more by momentary . . . conditions and constraints than by future requirements'.[9] The German view is reinforced by the organisation of British industrial firms, which are increasingly based on profit centres, their

6   Framework for Government Research and Development, 1972, Cmnd. 5046.
7   House of Lords, Select Committee on Science and Technology, Vol. 11, Evidence, p. 175.
8   Ibid., p. 54.
9   Dr Josef Rembser, *The Need for Reindustrialisation – Industrial Policy in the Federal Republic in Germany*, Tällberg Workshop, Sweden, 19–22 May 1982.

managers being rewarded with a bonus in accordance with profits. In short, the organisation reinforces the short-term outlook. The emphasis on the market is reflected in the composition of the Requirements Boards. Most of the Board members are industrialists; the numbers of academics are few. One Conservative Minister, when in charge of the Department, appeared to favour, as industrial members, young men who had made their riches quickly; these were not necessarily the people with the most forward view. Sir Peter Carey would have done better to phrase himself thus: 'In our work . . . we are trying all the time to get beyond the immediate market.' Hierarchically below the Department of Industry, or perhaps one ought to say in reality alongside it, there comes the British Technology Group, formed from an amalgamation of the National Enterprise Board (NEB) and the National Research and Development Corporation (NRDC). The NEB was established by a Labour Government to help finance enterprises which otherwise could not get off the ground; its most famous association is with Inmos, the micro-chip manufacturing firm, which will continue to require a high degree of capital. Even so, its share of the world's trade in micro-chips is only 4 per cent, contrasted with 50 per cent in the United States and 30 per cent in Japan. Still it could provide a platform for further developments. In 1983 the wings of the NEB were clipped, though in ways which are unclear and it is now concerned only with the continued running of enterprises earlier established. The apparent rationale is that the unfettered private sector will spontanteously invest in new technology. It is true that since the formation of Inmos there have come into being a number of capital venture firms prepared to take up equity in risky projects; whether they command sufficient capital as to render the NEB redundant is doubtful. NRDC, on the other hand, remains extant. The philosophy behind it is exactly the same as that behind the NEB but its financial sums are much smaller. It patents inventions emanating in the main from the universities, and in the pharmaceutical field it has been highly successful.

Finally there is the Procurement Executive of the Department of Defence, formed in 1971 and heir to the procurement functions formerly exercised by the Ministry of Supply. This development seems to have started with Sir Norman Brook, when examining my proposal for a Ministry of Technology. There does not appear to be much communication between the Procurement Executive and other technological organisations. Defence procurement appears to remain a kingdom unto itself.

There emerge then a number of seemingly disparate organisations: ACARD, effective but advisory only; the Requirement Boards, generally a failure; the British Technology Group, forced to remain subfusc; and the Procurement Executive of the Department of Defence, keeping itself unto itself. While so many groups cannot exist without the passage of some knowledge between one and the others, they work at different levels of time, the main distinction being between ACARD, looking to the future, and the Requirements Boards, immersed in the market – i.e. the present. Behind them all there appears to be no concerted purpose. Just as there was no energy policy, so also there is no policy for technology.

Such is not the situation in France. On the advent to power of M. Mitterand, he assembled the then various organisations into one Ministry – the Ministère pour la Recherche et la Technologie, later the Ministère pour la Receherche et l'Industrie. There are several points to be noted about this Ministry. First, the Minister is chairman of an inter-ministerial committee on science and technology, and thus has an indirect say in university work. Secondly, he is in charge of all science and technology policy. Thirdly, he places research and development contracts, presumably in the light of this policy, through ANVAR (Agence Nationale de Valorisation de la Recherche), which has regional offices. Fourthly, he has a unit with a remit of foreseeing future developments, auditing work done, and conducting research on research. Though the Minister has changed, there is no reason to believe that the Ministry has been unsucccessful. In parentheses it should perhaps be noted that the Ministry takes its view of future markets from the Commissariat au Plan, adapting its forward technology to markets as foreseen.

The situation in West Germany is different from that in France, primarily in the integration of defence with civil technology. The main instrument for the public financial support of all research and development is the Bundesministerium für Forschung und Technologie (BMFT). It proffers its support in two principal ways. First, it sponsors the 50 or so research institutes of the Max Planck Gesellschaft, founded to fill in gaps in university research, to unify university research, or to undertake research neglected in the universities. Alongside the Max Planck Gesellschaft is a small unit located at Munich – Garsching Instrumente – the staff of which regularly visits the 50 institutes and patents what it judges to be patentable.

Secondly, the BMFT sponsors applied technology through the

Fraunhofer Gesellschaft, comprising some 26 institutes. The institution was started in 1949, the initial finance coming from the Government, but with the stipulation that the more the Gesellschaft could obtain from industry, the greater would be the governmental contribution. To begin with, the institutes of the Fraunhofer Gesellschaft took the initiative in going out to industry, feeding it with ideas and proposals. So successful were they in this respect, that industry has increasingly come to them, submitting projects for evaluation. Sometimes the projects are modified, though the undertaking is under no obligation to accept the suggested changes. In so far as it accepts, it also receives financial aid.

The description illustrates a fundamental difference between the United Kingdom, on the one hand, and France and Germany on the other. 'In other advanced capitalist countries, especially France and Japan, there is a general tendency for administrations to push economic policies to operation levels which are more closely specified. The irrelevance of macro policy and the ineffectiveness of micro policy ensured that the British Government played a much more indirect role.'[10] The Britishers, allegedly pragmatic, believe in the free market; they see a clear distinction between the free market and centralised direction. The French and the Germans, allegedly ideological, are more pragmatic; they see a convergence. They believe that government can command a wider view than firms, whose gaze is fixed on the immediate ground. They therefore engage in a dialogue, in the course of which both sides may modify their views. This concept – planning by dialogue – is far removed from the customer supremacy on which British policy is reefed.

This difference of belief may explain the different amounts, which governments in different countries spend on research and development in the private sector. The differences are brought out in Table 1.

The table shows that spending on R and D by the United Kingdom is the lowest in the three countries in total terms. The lowness of the British figure may be better appreciated if account is taken of the volume of R and D spending on defence, as illustrated in Table 2.

It will be seen that British spending on defence R and D hovered around 50 per cent. In the technological field the Government's share

[10] Williams, Williams and Thomas, *Why are the British Bad at Manufacturing?* Routledge and Kegan Paul, London, 1983, p. 100.

Table 1 *Budget appropriations for R and D in 1982*

	Final R and D appropriations in 1982 at current values and exchange rates (million European units of account)		Ratio of R and D appropriations to total budget (%)	Ratio of R and D appropriations to GDP (%)
	Total	Civil		
Federal Republic of Germany	8,125	7,432	4.21	1.20
France	7,337	4,741	5.79	1.36
United Kingdom	6,550	3,263	3.19	1.36

Source: Eurostat, 1984, Table 1, p. 119

Table 2 *Defence spending as % of total financing*

	1975	1981	1982	1983 (provisional)
Federal Republic of Germany	11.0	8.8	8.5	8.4
France	29.8	32.5	35.4	33.0
United Kingdom	46.4	48.9	50.2	50.2

Source: Eurostat, 1984, Table IV, p. 124

in R and D spending fell from 16.0 per cent in 1981 to 14.3 per cent in 1982 and 1983 (the figure for the latter year being provisional). The most important aspect of the UK economy was thus subject to a degree of neglect.

The difference in the degrees of governmental financial support for civil R and D is reflected in comparative accomplishment. Take, for example, 'The number of 'developed' robots per 10,000 workers in 1980: Sweden = 8, Japan = 6, U.S.A. = 1.6, Germany = 1.1, Italy = 0.9, France = 0.7, United Kingdom = 0.3.'[11] Differences of definition

---

[11] Albert and R. J. Ball, *Towards European Economic Recovery in the 1980s*, European Parliament Working Documents, 1983, p. 27.

could account for the extent of the disparity shown, but scarcely for the fact of disparity.

Public help need not of course be given only by way of partial contributions, whether loans or grants, to research and development. For example, in Sweden the world-wide expenditure on research and development of Alfa-Laval is entirely financed by the Government.

Even though differences in the method of finance may distort the figures given, they do not obscure the fundamental difference between the United Kingdom and other countries. Nor do they illuminate the basic problem: can a government see the technological future better than a private firm? Or rather, can both see it together better than either in isolation?

Government has in general a closer knowledge of social trends than private firms. The social trends detected will after an interval translate themselves into consumers' needs. The satisfaction of these needs will require both a perception of a possible market and the perception of a technology to meet the market. Most examples of technological advance seem to suggest that the future is 'market pulled' rather than 'technologically pushed'. Alternatively, experts in a given technological field may be able to discern future developments, in which case technological advance is 'technologically pushed'. Whatever the truth the fact remains that a government can contribute a great deal to the firm's view of the future. To this extent government and the private sector are not in opposition to each other; they need to contrive instruments through which they can work together. Given the present organisation in Britain the best instrument would appear to be the British Technology Group, advised by ACARD.

The early post-war technologies – nuclear power, aircraft, large computers – required capital sums beyond the means of private firms; to the extent that this was so government perforce had to enter upon the scene. It may be said that we have now entered the age of the small computer, with less demands on the government purse. This may be true, but only partly so. The fifth frame computer, the production of the micro-chip, and possibly the development of bio-technology all require large capital sums. That is the basic case for government intervention, with smaller private industries swimming in the wake of that intervention. Without such intervention it is difficult to see how the country can overcome the basic weakness detected by the first Ministry of Technology – the tendency to export products of low added value and import products of higher added value.

12

THE VIEW FROM THE PRICES AND INCOMES BOARD: INCOMES

Macmillan had three Chancellors of the Exchequer: Heathcot Amory, Selwyn Lloyd and Reginald Maudling. All were Keynesian in the sense that they believed in the greater effectiveness of fiscal or budgetary as against monetary methods of regulating demand in the economy; they differed only in their degree of boldness.

Heathcot Amory made his views explicit in a letter to O. T. Falk dated 3 February 1961:

> The use we have made of monetary instruments has shown that . . . they are not either delicate or discriminating enough . . . the most effective instrument is the Budget and we have been trying for the last few years to get our people in Parliament (viz., the Conservatives) to accept its use as a balancing instrument as even more important than its purely financial role. Our party still regard this with some horror.[1]

The distinction between budgetary and monetary methods of regulating demand has been grossly exaggerated. Note that both are concerned with demand. Given this objective there has been over time a slight shift of emphasis from one method to the other. By the mid-1950s – that is, by the time Mr Macmillan became Chancellor of the Exchequer – Mr Macmillan and his three Chancellors were preoccupied with the problem of cost-push. Later there took place a change. As the seventies approached more and more people in the Treasury began to get worried about what was happening to the money supply and felt that the expansion of demand (through the budget) was not in fact reducing unemployment. It was for the simple reason that Britain was uncompetitive in its external trade; no mere expansion of domestic demand, however contrived, could have obviated the effect on unemployment of uncompetitiveness in trading.

---

[1]   Sir Harold Hartley, Papers, Archives Centre, Churchill College, Cambridge.

This change of view, which occurred a decade or so before Mrs Thatcher came to office, did not, however, rule out the phenomenon of cost-push. Nor did it come anywhere near to saying 'Only money matters.'

Heathcot Amory was not willingly prepared so to expand demand through the Budget that it induced inflation and thus aggravated a deficit in the balance of payments. He was, however, malleable in Mr Macmillan's hands and in the event this is exactly what he did – he aggravated the deficit in the balance of payments. It is clear from the earlier history that Mr Butler expanded demand, through a lowering of taxes, on the eve of the 1955 Election and that Mr Macmillan himself encouraged increased Government spending on the eve of the 1959 Election. Heathcot Amory could not resist him. As for Selwyn Lloyd, he was too adventurous. As against a long-term trend of an increase in output of 2½–3 per cent a year, he wanted to aim at a rate of growth of 5 per cent. With difficulty he was persuaded by officials to bring back his target to 4 per cent. Reginald Maudling also adhered to the same target of 4 per cent. Both, in other words, pursued a policy of faster growth, and hoped to contain any inflationary effects through an 'incomes policy'.

But why an incomes policy? Keynes had formed the view that a depression did not automatically right itself, except possibly after a very long interval, because of the inflexibility of a primarily monopolistic economy. Both wages and prices were 'sticky' downwards. The fact is confirmed even in the recession of the 1980s.[2] And added testimony has been given by Lord Cockfield.

> We suffer in this country, from market domination, price leadership, parallel pricing, the lack of effective competition, unwillingness to compete on price, which in many trades is regarded as disreputable or undesirable, and a 'cost plus' mentality under which the instinctive reaction to cost increases is to pass them on in price, rather than absorb them in greater efficiency, with the resulting erosion of resistance to cost increases, particularly unjustified increases in labour costs . . . it is not so much the active and deliberate abuse which is the problem as a general attitude of uncompetitiveness.[3]

This means that a contraction of demand, whether brought about either through the budget or through some other route, had its primary reflection in reduced output rather than in reduced wages and

[2]   *The Observer*, 26 February 1984, p. 32.
[3]   Sir Arthur Cockfield, 'The Price Commission and the Price Control', *The Three Banks Review*, March 1978, No. 17.

prices. It was a natural reciprocal of this view that the expansion which Governments contrived, mainly for electoral reasons, could proceed without inflation provided that wages and prices were also 'sticky' upwards – that is, did not rise faster than output.

The Macmillan Government's expansion plans, coupled with its inability to contain wages and prices, left the incoming Labour Government of 1964 with a horrendous legacy, the balance of payments being in deficit to the tune of some £800 million. Devaluation was considered but put aside. Three years later, in 1967, it became inevitable. It was slow, however, to pay off. Devaluation required that resources be diverted from home use to export. The Labour Government's initial reaction to devaluation was to cut spending; since Government spending was mainly for capital purposes, the results were tardy. It was only in 1968, when Mr Roy Jenkins raised taxes and thus quickly, and adversely, affected consumption, that the switch of resources took place. By 1969, as the Labour Government approached its end, devaluation was beginning to pay off.

In the interim I had played a part which I could not evade. Mr Harold (now Lord) Wilson, having two strong characters in Mr Callaghan and Mr (later Lord) George Brown, divided the economic function between them. The short-term or financial function was given to Mr Callaghan at the Treasury, the long-term or real resources function to Mr George Brown at the new Department of Economic Affairs.

It is fair to add that this distinction of function was due to more than the presence of two powerful personalities. There was a feeling that the long term had been sacrificed to the short term and that there should be a will to over-ride short term crises in the balance of payments if one was to strengthen an uncompetitive British industry. This, after all, was what Mr Maudling had attempted. There remained, however, the fact that the country was prone to periodic crises in the balance of payments, whatever the reasons might be, and that each crisis as it arose had to be dealt with and overcome before the deeper problems of British industry could be attended to. This ineluctable truth meant that the Treasury remained the primary economic Department. And it was its primacy in dealing with a short-term crisis which ultimately brought about the downfall of the DEA. The truth is that the long term is a succession of shorter terms and the short term simply cannot be over-ridden.

Mr George Brown none the less bravely followed essentially the same policy as his Conservative predecessors – expansion at the rate of 4 per cent a year with a constraint on wages and prices. The difference was that the constraint on prices and incomes was much more formidable. There was set up a new body – the National Board for Prices and Incomes (NBPI).

The creation of the Board followed on a Statement of Intent in which the Government, the employers and the trade unions all pledged themselves to improve productivity and to exercise restraint in raising incomes and prices. The statement was in effect the attainment of a consensus, all three bodies committing themselves to a common objective. Against the background of British economic history, a history of conflict between contending parties, the Statement was a unique achievement, possible only to a George Brown, a person of tremendous vision and courage, marred by great defects. I read about the Statement of Intent incredulously in Washington. Back in London I found that to chair the National Board, Mr Brown, inspired by his Prime Minister, included my name, without my knowing it, in a list submitted to the CBI (then the FBI) and the TUC. Unbelieving, I first learned of the fact through the press. Only when I was summoned to see Mr George Brown did the truth begin to dawn. Mine, so I was told, was the only name accepted by both employers and trade unionists. This alone would have made it impossible to refuse the invitation.

But there were also other reasons for acceptance. The challenge was much greater than that set me by Mr Macmillan, who, when I turned, after the manner of ex-Ministers, into a back-bench critic, offered me the chairmanship of the new Covent Garden Marketing Authority, with some 'elevation of status'. The most compulsive reason, however, was that Keynesianism had opened up a new economic world, requiring new institutions. In this sense I could be a pioneer.

Few, however, recognised the significance of the new institution. The pre-Keynesian view of the economy was that it was basically competitive and that the natural state of affairs was full employment. In this competition the worker, lacking financial reserves, was ill matched against the capitalist. He had therefore to be fortified by the removal of restrictions against his combining with others. The resulting combination or union was encouraged to bargain with individual employers or an employers' association in the relevant industry. Where the combination was non-existent or weak legal wage boards known as wages councils were set up to simulate the results of negotiation and to establish minimum wages. There was a Wages Councils

Act as late as 1959. Similarly in public employment, where the Government was likely to be the dominant party in any negotiation, special review bodies were established to determine remuneration, ostensibly objectively. The purpose of all these measures was to establish an equality in the bargaining process. Finally, to avert the risk of industrial disruption should bargaining break down, there was an arbitration court or a special court of inquiry. There was thus a state-supported structure designed to uphold the tradition of collective bargaining. Amidst this welter of institutions the primary role of the Ministry of Labour was that of a conciliator. When the Conservatives were returned to office in 1970 one of the first remarks made to me by Mr Robert (now Lord) Carr, effectively the new Minister of Labour, was that he was determined to restore to the Ministry its conciliating function.

On to this antediluvian, in the sense of pre-Keynesian, world there was suddenly obtruded the National Board for Prices and Incomes working to rules, albeit loose, laid down for it by the Government. How were the new and the old to be reconciled the one with the other? The Drapery Wages Council, for example, felt that it was debarred by the 1959 Wages Councils Act from taking into consideration anything other than the need to increase the statutory minimum remuneration to a reasonable level. Should arbitration bodies be required to work to the same rules as the Board? Should review bodies have a degree of common membership with the Board, or at least a common secretariat? In spite of all the talk little was done. The Board was inevitably constrained by the continued existence of bodies preceding it in birth. Its greatest difficulty was with the attitude of arbitration panels, which saw their role as the promotion of industrial peace rather than the promotion of competitive labour costs.

What had happened was that, while Keynes had effected a revolution in thinking, there was no revolution in institutions. They went on as before, unaffected. Government, the creator of such institutions, still lagged in general behind the times.

In addition Mr George Brown's long-term plan, which the Board was designed to sustain, collapsed. Its objectives were made unrealistic by the measures taken to deal with the long-drawn-out balance of payments crisis. The failure of the plan was not in itself a condemnation of planning; it was but an illustration of the fact that when the foreign exchange reserves are threatened the threat is given precedence above all else. The destruction of the plan heralded the destruction of the Department of Economic Affairs itself. A penultimate thrust of the knife was delivered by George Brown himself. Less than two years after he had founded the DEA he moved to the Foreign Office. As Foreign Secretary he insisted that the co-ordination of external financial policy be moved from the DEA to the Cabinet Office. After that prices and incomes were the one task left for the DEA.

The Board none the less went on for five and a half years until the Conservative Government returned in 1970 ordered its demise. I had been warned of the intention by the American consultants to whom Mr Heath, when in Opposition, turned for advice. The Board produced in all some 170 reports. True, some reports treated the same subject more than once. Nonetheless, the view obtained of British industry was the most comprehensive that I know.

The Board's task was to prevent the opportunity for full employment opened up by Keynes from being defeated. For this purpose it had to help with other instruments to conquer inflation, or rising prices, the then rate of increase being 3 per cent a year. There are three main components to prices; the costs of raw materials, the incomes of employees and the rate of profit sought. Raw materials are invariably imported; their prices reflect therefore a world price; and given an act of devaluation, such as that in 1967, imported raw material prices rise; that rise has inevitably to be incorporated in domestic prices, for it is one of the purposes of devaluation to deter imports. Raw material prices may therefore be disregarded. The important problems surround incomes and the rate of profit sought. The relationship between them can be both positive and negative. It is positive if incomes rise in response to rising profits, whether retained in the business or distributed to shareholders, or if employers enjoying rising profits, are more generous in income payments to employees. On the other hand, the relationship is negative if incomes rise at the expense of profits, and in general that would appear to have been the case. In Britain 'The underlying profit trend appears to have been downward for over 100 years.'[4]

When the Board came into existence wage rates were rising at a rate of about 7.5 per cent a year, while output per man was rising at a rate of only 1.5 per cent a year. Why was there this discrepancy? The popular view is that trade unions had become too powerful. This view is too

[4]   Matthews, Feinstein and Odling-Smee, *British Economic Growth 1856–1973*, Stanford University Press, 1982, p. 500.

simplistic. Trade unions had come into being because other agencies in the economy chose to exercise power; the role of the trade unions was to act as a countervailing power. This, after all, was the reason for their being and the legal sub-structure which supported them. Powerful trade unions and powerful employers' organisations can after all between them beneficially regulate the economy, as in Sweden and in Austria. But such is not the case in Britain. It was noted earlier that Lord Citrine, when General Secretary of the TUC, had failed to move the unions towards centralised bargaining and that he had resigned when the TUC General Council refused to endorse a proposal to establish regional TUC offices. It might be argued that trade unions are potentially powerful in an injurious sense when they combine together, as the NUM sought in 1984, but even then differences between the unions made an alliance difficult, and the so-called Triple Alliance became dubbed the 'cripple Alliance'. Further, as was said of the London Brick Company, which was responsible for 90 per cent of the output of fletton bricks, 'the market power of the company is transmitted to the trade unions' (Cmnd. 4422, para. 58). It was not the exercise of power by trade unions which struck the Board. On the contrary, in more than one instance, the Board found that unions were fragmented in various ways; the fragmentation led to competition between unions or between different groups of union members; and the competition in turn led to a contribution to inflation. In other words, unions had taken on the ethos of the surrounding capitalist environment, acting as private enterprise is supposed to act. A similar phenomenon was found on the employers' side, one bank, for example, acting without regard for the effect on other banks.

Several examples may be cited of competition between unions. It was found in the Report on Prices of Bread and Flour (Cmnd. 2760) that there were five unions and that as a result of geographical competition one area tried to obtain more than another. Similarly, in the Report on Pay and Conditions of Service of Engineering Workers (Cmnd. 3945) bargaining was undertaken by one group without regard for the implications for other groups. As a result supervisors could be paid less than the average of those whom they supervised, the skilled less than the unskilled, and the qualified less than the unqualified. Yet again, in the Report on Pay Awards made by the City and Council of Bristol to Staff Employed in its Dock Undertaking (Cmnd. 3732), it was found that negotiations were undertaken first with the labourers, and only later with the craftsmen. It was inevitable that the craftsmen should aim for a higher increase than that granted to the labourers.

Nor was it only in the private sector that fragmented bargaining took place. In the National Health Service, for example, the pay of nurses was pronounced upon by Professor Asa Briggs, that of hospital scientific and technical staff by Lord Zuckerman, and that of the hospital pharmaceutical service by Sir Noel Hall.

High pay could occur without trade unions. For instance, in the Report on Office Staff Employment Agencies: Charges and Salaries (Cmnd. 3828) it was found that 'The payment of office staff which has not been subject to collective bargaining to the same extent as in other fields of employment has increased sharply.' Similarly in the Report on Pay and Conditions in the Civil Engineering Industry (Cmnd. 3836) 'the level of trade union activity was low'. It might have been the expanding economy, more than trade unions, which made for fast-rising pay. In general the causes of the accelerating post-war inflation remain uncertain. The war itself may have given rise to high expectations, expectations subsequently reinforced by social developments such as television, with its pictures, real or imaginary, of life in high society. Unions could have been instruments in a national mood.

Nor could they have acted effectively without the connivance of management. Inefficiencies on the part of management were found to be widespread. In, for example, the Report on Job Evaluation (Cmnd. 3772) 'only seven of 91 companies approached knew what the change in their wage bills had been following the introduction of a job evaluation scheme'. In the Report on Pay and Productivity in the Car Delivery Industry (Cmnd. 3929) 'not one firm costed with any accuracy the increase in wage rates which resulted from the negotiations in Birmingham last year'. Finally, in the Report on Hours and Overtime in the London Clearing Banks (Cmnd. 4301) 'the banks do not appear to have made any firm estimate of future staff levels to be expected after the completion of the computerisation programme'.

It was management that was ultimately responsible for fragmented bargaining. As the Fourth General Report (Cmnd. 4130) put it: 'Our general experience is that the crucial factor in raising productivity is almost always the quality of management and management control.' Yet there were exceptions to a generally sorry tale. The Report of Pay and Conditions of Craftsmen in Imperial Chemical Industries Ltd (Cmnd. 3941) noted: 'I.C.I. has long made effective use of such techniques as work study and job evaluation which are now being introduced in some parts of British industry, so that standards of labour efficiency in the company can be shown to be good compared with standards at large.'

When trade unions or parts of trade unions and employers or parts of employers' associations indulged in bargaining, what criterion did they have in mind? The dominant criterion was comparison with somebody else. Just as one group in a plant sought comparison with another group, so an industry might seek comparison with other industries, the comparison often being based on a formula, derived possibly from an earlier inquiry. Thus railwaymen based their comparisons with basic rates in other industries as set out in the Pay Inquiry (Guillebaud) Report of 1960 (Pay and Conditions of British Railways Staff, Cmnd. 2873). The armed forces used a Grigg (after Sir James Grigg) formula established in 1958 and based on a comparison with Civil Service pay (Armed Forces Pay, Cmnd. 2881). The London busmen and their employers used a Phelps Brown (after Sir Henry Phelps Brown) formula (Pay and Conditions of Busmen, Cmnd. 3012). In other cases trade unions invented their own formula, the Association of University Teachers, for example, seeking 'comparability' with the pay levels of university graduates who had entered walks of life other than the universities (Standing Reference on the Pay of University Teachers in Great Britain Cmnd. 3866). Whenever a pay increase was agreed to on grounds of 'comparability', it was always in the commercial sector passed on in increased prices.

The claim for 'comparability', whether with other groups within a plant or firm or with other industries lay in a search for equity or 'fairness'. As such it was understandable. It arose in part from efforts by management to provide incentives to workers to increase output. The traditional form of incentive was an extra payment to an individual or small group if output exceeded a certain target. This inevitably meant that some individuals were paid more than others.

> Our studies suggested that conventional P.B.R. (Payment by Results) had contributed to drift (i.e. an excess of earnings over basic rates nationally agreed upon) both directly and by disturbing wage differential within the enterprise which led to pressures for further wage increases, although the actual amount of drift resulting directly from P.B.R. systems which were under firm control was generally limited to 1 or 2 per cent a year.

Where there was no effective management control, as in the majority of cases,

> Our estimates suggested that over several recent years up to about half the annual increase in the average hourly earnings of manual workers might be attributed to wage drift, which meant that the drift had averaged up to some 4 per cent a year, which alone . . . exceeded the normal average growth in productivity. (Payment by Results Systems, Cmnd. 3627)

In short, traditional payment by results systems, designed to improve output, were generally, with few exceptions, counter-productive in the sense of being also inflationary.

In the 1950s an attempt was made to escape from the evils of traditional incentive schemes by more broadly based 'productivity agreements' covering the greater part, if not the whole, of a plant or a firm. The pioneering company in this respect was Esso. It was followed by the Electricity Supply Industry, ICI, British Oxygen and Alcan. The 'productivity agreement' had the virtue of being reasonably comprehensive, thus overcoming, or at least mitigating, the effects of fragmentation. On the other hand, it had its potential dangers. It could theoretically lead to high earnings in one firm which could be copied by another firm, but without necessarily any increase in productivity. 'From the agreements looked at, we found little evidence to suggest that a genuine productivity agreement had an inflationary effect outside the plant in which it was concluded; though it is possible that a wide extension of productivity agreements, particularly if some of them are not wholly genuine, might yield a different conclusion' (Productivity Agreements, Cmnd. 3311). This is exactly what happened. Productivity agreements became a vogue, designed, under weak managements, to elude the incomes policy. They appeared in such large numbers that they were 'vetted' by the Ministry of Labour (later baptised as the Department of Employment), an organisation ill equipped for the task. Thus they fell into disrepute. Even so, the statistics show that the emphasis on productivity had for a time a positive effect. The basic problem of pay bargaining – how to reconcile efficiency with equity – thus remained for the time being unsolved.

What was surprising was the failure of individual managements, analogous to the failure of groups of workers, to understand the implications of their actions for others. In a letter to the Board dated 28 June 1965, Mr Thackstone, then General Manager of the Midland Bank, wrote 'we find it difficult to understand why other parties should be consulted in any way about a subject that rests confidentially between the Bank and the recognised negotiating body of its own staff'. Yet the pay agreement reached by the Midland Bank quickly had its repercussions on other clearing banks. The Midland Bank had not understood that there was a public interest in every individual bargain. The electricity industry reacted in a not dissimilar fashion when it was proposed that the Board should undertake studies of the efficiency of nationalised industries as an accompaniment to the examination of their prices. The electricity industry commented that an inquiry would be better undertaken by consultants as owing a 'loyalty or duty to the industry'.

A singular but important claim was made by the Brewers' Society, commenting on the Board's first Report on beer prices (Costs, Prices and Profits in the Brewing Industry, Cmnd. 2965) which had noted that the production bonuses paid bore, as usual, little relationship to productivity. The Society's commentary read: 'if Government policy leads to a large excess demand for labour it is not reasonable to expect a single industry to put up an effective resistance to wage claims'. The commentary appeared to be inspired by the Economists' Advisory Group, chaired by Professor Victor Morgan. Yet ICI had labour costs under control whatever the state of demand. So did the Film Processing Industry (Pay of Certain Employees in the Film Processing Industry, Cmnd. 4185). A basic weakness lay with individual managements and was obscured by the preoccupation of economists with macro-economic policy.

The phrase 'a large excess demand for labour' is in fact meaningless. When exactly does the demand for labour cease to be excessive? When prices are finally constant, with the rate of unemployment at 13 per cent or higher? The phrase also conceals many things. In an early Report on Pay and Conditions of Busmen (Cmnd. 3012) it was found that manpower shortage was measured by reference to the establishment, which declined as the demand for the use of buses declined. Again, in the Report on the Pay of Nurses and Midwives in the National Health Service (Cmnd. 3581), it was ascertained that shortages of staff were not general but were concentrated in particular grades, particular types of hospital, and at particular periods of the week and the day. It was to these particular areas that pay increases should be confined. Corresponding to the failure to identify particular areas of shortage was a failure to tap particular sources of supply, such as women, immigrants and part-time workers (Report on Pay of Municipal Busmen, Cmnd. 3605).

Were trade unions in general obstructive to technical change, and thus contributors to rising costs and prices? The evidence before the Board is ambiguous. In the case of the bread-making industry, in which, it was suggested, a change in manning practices could lead to a containment of costs and prices, 'no progress had been made by either side of the industry in securing a more effective deployment of labour' (Prices of Bread and Flour, Cmnd. 2760 and Wages in the Bakery Industry, Cmnd, 3019). On the other hand, by and large, there appeared to be a readiness to accept new techniques so long as they did not lead to redundancy. In some cases there could be no doubt about the readiness to accept new techniques. In, for example, the Report on the Pay of Staff Workers in the Gas Industry (Cmnd. 3795) it was written: 'this is an industry willing to try out new ideas ... Area Boards have made worthwhile savings through their use and ... staffs have willingly co-operated.' In like terms the Report on the Pay of Certain Employees in the Film Processing Industry (Cmnd. 4185) noted the 'employees' readiness to adapt their working practices to technical change'. Finally, in the case of the Bristol Dock Undertaking 'our enquiries showed that, as a result of co-operation and flexibility by the staff, there had been increased productivity in part reflected in a reduction in the number of staff' (Pay Awards Made by the City and County of Bristol to Staff Employed in its Dock Undertaking, Cmnd. 3752).

Where there was a resistance to change it was associated with a feeling of uncertainty or alternatively a long memory of unemployment. The Report on Costs and Revenues of Independent Television Companies (Cmnd. 4524) inferred from the fact that three companies had lost their franchises in 1968 a general feeling of insecurity among employees and possibly a hardening of union attitudes to technical change. The most striking case of resistance to change was among the busmen of Dundee, who refused, even temporarily, to operate high-capacity double-decker buses on routes normally served by middle-capacity buses (Report on Pay and Conditions of Busmen Employed by the Corporation of Dundee, Cmnd. 3791). Dundee had experienced an unemployment rate of 30 per cent in the inter-war years. Did the memory of this fact explain the refusal? A lesson to other companies was contained in the Report on the General Accident Company, 'the Group had embarked on a number of schemes designed to improve ... its use of manpower. This had been done without prior consultation with the staff, which might have accounted for the feelings of insecurity of some of the experienced staff' (Salaries of Staff Employed by the General Accident Fire and Life Assurance Corporation Limited, Cmnd. 3398). In sum, resistance to change is greater the greater the feeling of insecurity.

Mancur Olson attributes national decline to the organisations which attempt in a stable society to secure for themselves and maximum distribution of income.[5] Plenty of examples of such organisations were found. The building societies, for instance, recommended rates which kept in being the inefficient and led the more efficient to maintain higher reserves than were necessary (Report on Building Societies, Cmnd. 3136); the charge for conveyancing by solicitors was determined by an external body which left the individual solicitor free to go above the scale, but not below it (Report on Remuneration of Solicitors, Cmnd. 3529); the Royal Institute of British Architects sought to enforce on all architects a minimum scale of charges, on the whole not unsuccessfully (Report on Architects Costs and Fees, Cmnd. 3653); and the Ministry of Agriculture, in fixing the price of milk, averaged costs, with the result that the London milk distributor, who incurred higher costs of processing, earned less than his provincial counterpart (Report on the Remuneration of Milk Distributors, Cmnd. 3477).

All this was challengeable and to a certain degree there has since been change. But did it really amount to much compared with the general poverty of management in both private and public sectors? As the Report on Pay and Conditions in the Building Industry (Cmnd. 3837) put it: 'productivity is not simply a question of the right payment system; no system will work well if it is poorly managed. The first essential step therefore is to raise the standard of management.' But how?

The Donovan Commission on Trade Unions, sitting around this time, had noticed that the determination of wages had passed from national negotiators to individual plants. In so far as Mrs Thatcher's Government has a view on the determination of wages in the private sector, it would likewise seem to lie in favour of bargaining at the plant. In the Board's experience plant bargaining meant bargaining at different times with different groups of workers, each group seeking to jump over the other.

The answer to the resulting inflation lay in comprehensive bargain-

[5]   *The Rise and Decline of Nations*, Yale University Press, New Haven, 1982.

ing, or the simultaneous bargaining with all groups. This was more easily contrived when the plant was part of a large company; company bargaining could be comprehensive bargaining. The development was more difficult when companies were numerous and small, though not utterly impossible. The Report on Pay and Conditions in the Electrical Construction Industry (Cmnd. 4097) observed that the industry had established a Joint Industry Board, comprising a permanent body of experts to guide and advise the industry and responsible both to unions and managements. In the same way the Report on the Pay of Certain Employees in the Film Processing Industry (Cmnd. 4185) noted that rates centrally laid down had been generally adhered to and it was therefore better for negotiations to continue at the industry level.

R. J. Liddle and W. E. J. McCarthy have written: 'The real distinction between the Donovan view and the Board is that with the latter final responsibility for the regulation of earnings is supposed to rest with the national machinery, whereas in the Royal (i.e. Donovan) Commission's case responsibility is acknowledged to have shifted elsewhere.'[6] This statement is not strictly true. The Board was well aware of the shift, but it was also aware of the consequences – fragmented bargaining. The Board's aim was comprehensiveness. Had management at the plant been able to develop comprehensiveness in bargaining, the Board would have been happy to see negotiations remain at the plant. But there is no evidence that such a development has taken place. It was also recognised that comprehensiveness was not easily attained at the national level, in spite of the occasional exception. The most likely organisation to develop comprehensive bargaining was the company.

Some progress indeed appears to have been made at this level. But it is difficult to be certain, for there is now no official monitoring body. The Board set out to change institutions and practices; its recommendations, which were invariably for the longer term, needed to be followed up. Mrs Castle, during her tenure as Secretary of State of Employment, set up in her Department a division concerned with following up the Board's recommendations. But it has gone. Mrs Castle was an active Minister. On receiving undesired advice, she would burst into tears, thus melting the heart of the most hard-boiled official.

---

6 R. J. Liddle and W. E. J. McCarthy, 'The Impact of the Prices and Incomes Board on the Reform of Collective Bargaining', *British Journal of Industrial Relations*, 10, 412–39.

It was quite an effective method of getting her way. It was her misfortune to reach the office of Employment after the delay in devaluing, before it had time to show its effects, and faith in a prices and incomes policy was beginning to waver. But nobody could have done more to try to strengthen it, despite her later obsession with the will-o'-the-wisp of union power, as shown in 'In Place of Strife', a document submitted by her to the Cabinet but rejected.

It has, I trust, been established that the nature of wage bargaining has an upward effect on prices, and the nature is not changed whatever the level of demand. At the same time it has to be recognised that the task of reconciling efficiency with equity is extremely difficult, requiring careful study and calculation. Weak managements have a tendency to clutch at the straws of contemporary fashions, as determined by consultants, without regard to the implications of their actions for others.

So much for wages and their effects on prices. But what about other aspects of management which might affect prices and, in particular, the rate of profit sought?

13

THE VIEW FROM THE PRICES AND INCOMES BOARD: PRICES

British firms, as observed by the Board, were inclined on several counts to pitch prices higher than they needed to. They took into account, for example, costs not yet incurred – for example, a wage settlement which it was intended to make but which had not yet been agreed upon. As the Board expressed the trait in its Report on Electricity and Gas Tariffs (Cmnd. 2862) 'whilst it is appropriate when considering price increases to take into account prospective as well as past costs, a distinction should be drawn between those costs which it is known are going to occur and those increases which simply assume a rate of cost of inflation similar to that known in the past'. A tax like that of the Selective Employment tax, intended by the Labour Government of 1964–70 to divert labour from distribution to production, was similarly seized upon to raise prices more than the tax warranted.

There was also a conservatism in the price structure. Courtaulds, for example, submitted proposals for a general increase in a price list which had not changed for many years and did not reflect the current differences in production costs. When this was pointed out the company amended its application and lowered the average price increase sought (Report on Man-made Fibre and Cotton Yard Prices, Cmnd. 4092). Likewise, the Report of Electric Motor Prices (Cmnd. 4258) noted that 'There remains about the discount structure a considerable element of tradition and custom.' Also in the Report on Coal Prices (First Report) (Cmnd. 4255), it was observed that the coal price structure had been largely unchanged since 1951. Not for the first time it appeared that private and public sectors were similar rather than dissimilar.

Then there was a tendency to raise prices in accord with rising unit costs as the use of equipment was lowered. As the Report on the Prices of Standard Newsprint (Cmnd. 3210) put it, 'This was the first of several references raising the question of whether or not prices should be increased as a result of an increase in unit costs following a decline in demand.' Sidney Pollard has generalised this phenomenon, remarking that 'prices always rose most in periods of stagnation',[1] a statement which he statistically justifies.

Nor was competition, even where it prevailed, strong enough to counter these tendencies. In soap and detergents 'the major competitors are reasonably well matched in financial strength and it will rarely be possible for one of them to expand at the other's expense' (Prices of Household and Toilet Soaps, Soap Powders and Soapflakes and Soapless Detergents, Cmnd. 2791). Similarly, in aluminium semi-manufacturers, 'There was strong competition through service in all its forms, but no open, though some concealed, price cutting' (Costs and Prices of Aluminium Semi-Manufactures, Cmnd. 3378). The Monopolies and Mergers Commission has commented on the absence of price competition in terms which see a counterpart to the phenomenon of 'comparability' in wages, indicating that co-ordinated behaviour by firms 'whether by leadership or parallelism was a fairly widespread phenomenon.'[2]

The most difficult problem facing the Board on prices was the determination of the appropriate remuneration to capital. It was handed no definition in its terms of reference, unlike the Prices Commission set up in 1973 which had to have regard to the margin earned on total sales as compared with that obtaining at an earlier period. The Board had to develop its own definition. It was at first inclined to adopt the then practice of the Monopolies Commission, comparing the rate of return on capital invested with that found elsewhere. This practice was defective in several respects. The rate of return elsewhere was no criterion of what was appropriate if the rate of return in general was low; nor was a reasonably uniform rate of return necessarily desirable – a growing firm or industry should rightly enjoy a higher rate of return than the average; and the averaging of the rate of return conferred an unjustifiable benefit on some. Thus the Ministry of Agriculture based the price of milk on an average of costs (The Remuneration of Milk Distributors, Cmnd. 3477). Costs of processing milk in London were abnormally high, so that provincial distributors of milk were

---

[1]   Pollard, *The Wasting of the British Economy*, Croom Helm, London, 1982, p. 52.

[2]   Monopolies and Mergers Commission, Report on Parallel Pricing, Cmnd. 5330, 1973.

guaranteed an income to cover a higher level of costs than they actually incurred. The Ministry of Agriculture was a classic example of a Government Department acting in the same way as a private sector cartel. There is no indication that it has since changed its policy.

The Board accordingly shifted its ground, its standard practice being to compare the return on new investment, discounted to present-day values, with the cost of raising capital, the cost depending on the proportion of the total capital raised by way of loan, the proportion of profit retained in the business, and the proportion raised by way of equity capital with a varying rate of return. If the cost of capital, appropriately weighted according to the manner in which it was raised, exceeded the discounted rate of return, then a price increase was warranted.

Conversely, if the rate of return was considerably above the cost of capital the price increase asked for was disallowed. A famous instance was Portland Cement Prices (Cmnd. 3381). The estimated cost of finance over the next few years was 8 or 9 per cent; the price increase asked for would give a return on new investment of 12 per cent. It was considered that this would not have been consistent with the 'modest margin of profit' judged to be justifiable by the Restrictive Practices Court as a condition for upholding the common price agreement between firms.

Even the formula of comparing the cost of capital with the discounted return on new investment, which on the whole was acceptable to firms, since their estimate of the return was normally accepted, could not always be applied. In the case of viscose yarn, for example, demand was static, so that there was no need for new investment. If, however, a price increase were denied, then there was a danger of closed plants and therefore increased imports. A price increase was accordingly given for balance of payments reasons.

There were cases of firms which did not assess the discounted return on new investment. Such a case was the London Brick Company. In such an instance there was no alternative but to look at the historical return on assets, and compare with it the expected return as a result of the proposed price increase.

The Board's aim then was to maintain investment even while incomes were under restraint. Clearly, profit and investment could be sustained with greater efficiency. An example of its approach has been well cited by Mr Peter Maunder.

There is always the objection that price control is to be disliked because of interference in the freedom of firms to conduct their affairs as they see fit. Mr [A. J.] felt that the investigation of the Board into the bread industry was not 'undue interference with freedom to determine prices, it was rather an invitation to management to keep stricter control over its costs'.[3]

The Board then was out to increase efficiency. But it had no power to enforce efficiency; all it could do was to approve or disapprove of a proposed increase in price. What it could do was to point to areas of possible improvement. A particular inefficiency was in marketing. It has been noted that advanced technological projects in aircraft and nuclear power suffered from poor marketing. Weakness in marketing was in fact a national trait, which probably subsists even today. Thus the Report on Costs and Prices of Aluminium Semi-manufactures (Cmnd. 3378) noted that expenditure on marketing was half what it was in the United States. Spending on marketing by Ever Ready, the battery makers, was similarly low. And the Second Report on Coal Prices (Cmnd. 4455) questioned whether technical research and development and market research were closely related to each other.

Other areas of weakness were the multiplicity of varieties produced, leading to short production runs (Prices of Bread and Flour, Cmnd.2760); excessive stocks (Prices of Non-Alloy Bright Steel Bars, Cmnd. 4093); and too much wastage in the production process (Costs and Revenues of National Newspapers, Cmnd. 3455 and Cmnd. 4277).

It was the pervasive inefficiency which prompted Mrs Barbara Castle, who in 1968 had assumed responsibility for the prices and incomes policy, to propose the amalgamation of the NBPI and the Monopolies Commission to form a Commission for Industry and Manpower (CIM). I was the chairman-designate. The existence of a separate Monopolies Commission implies that any firm which has a monopoly (however that is defined) is potentially evil, while firms in a state of competition with each other are assumed to be in grace. ICI, a monopoly, at any rate in some fields, was found by the Board to be efficient, while firms in a state of competition did not necessarily compete in price. An independent testimony has been expressed by Mr Richard Shaw, of the University of Stirling.

[3]   Peter Maunder, *The Bread Industry in the United Kingdom*, University of Nottingham, Department of Agriculture and Horticulture.

The individual firm and industry studies by the N.B.P.I. and the Price Commission [a later body] have shown that there are often areas of inefficiency in firms which do not seem to be eliminated by competition . . . while accepting that competitive pressures will often both force firms to search continually for cost savings and make price controls unnecessary, it is naive to think that such pressure will always be adequate. The argument just stated suggests that there is a continuing role for some form of . . . efficiency monitoring agency.[4]

This is exactly what the CIM was supposed to be. Alas, Parliament was dissolved in 1970 before the bill creating the CIM had completed its passage.

The election of 1970 was won, as I had expected, by Mr Heath. While I knew of his intention to abolish the NBPI, I thought it just possible that, on the assumption of power, he might change his mind. After all, I had never understood his attitude in the years immediately preceding and following his advent to power in 1970. It clearly stemmed from Conservative gatherings held at Selhurst Park, Croydon, from which fact arose the description 'Selsdon' Conservatism. At any rate, this attitude appeared alien both to the Heath I knew before and the Heath I knew after. We had seen each other fairly regularly during my time at the NBPI. He had never on these occasions sought my views on the NBPI or the CIM. President Nixon's Council of Economic Advisers, on the other hand, did, when incomes and prices controls were introduced in August 1971. Nor had Mr Heath, in my presence, expressed any views himself.

It was not Mr Heath himself, however, who killed the NBPI, it was the late Iain Macleod. Treasury officials emphasised to him the importance of continuing both the NBPI and myself as Chairman. The reaction was hostile and I was duly warned of the fact. I thereupon took my leave of the Board. Macleod, the Chancellor, unlike the Macleod at the Ministry of Labour, was initially a simplistic 'monetarist', with no conception of the multiple causes of inflation. Whether he would have changed, as Mr Heath later changed, no one will ever know. But I doubt whether he ever had a firm economic view – he followed the fashion, but without fully understanding it.

Nemesis visited Mr Heath two years later. Faced with rising unemployment, he panicked. Taxes were cut, spending was increased, and

---

4   Richard Shaw, 'Price Controls and Inflation', *Economics*, 16, Part 4, No. 72, Winter 1980.

pay and price controls were introduced. But they were far different from the 'controls' drawn up by Labour. As Sir William (later Lord) Armstrong put it to me: 'Officials were under an instruction to make the new organisation appear as different as possible from the old.' Instead of one NBPI, there were established two boards, one for pay and one for prices. Both were copies, straight from American practice. Although I had recommended a single board, the US Administration believed in a separate board for prices. This belief rested on the assumption that prices, in addition to reflecting rising wage costs, were 'administered' – in other words, companies were powerful enough to impose their prices on the consumer rather than passively accept prices determined in a market. Both the new British Boards were required to operate to far more rigid rules than those which had governed the NBPI. In other words, the controls were tighter under the Conservatives than under Labour. And the pre-tax return on capital invested rapidly fell – from an average of 8.8 per cent in 1970–3 to 6.1 per cent in 1979.[5] Not until 1979, when a former Secretary to the NBPI, Sir Kenneth Clucas, was Permanent Secretary to the Department of Prices and Consumer Protection, were the terms of reference of the Price Commission modified to make it morre like the NBPI. Two years later, when the Conservatives returned to office, it was abolished, just as Labour had abolished the Pay Board in 1974.

What both parties failed to recognise was the investigative usefulness of the NBPI. It had a relatively small Board, but a largish staff – some 250 – trained in investigation. By contrast, a Royal Commission or a Departmental Committee, has a largish top structure, but a minuscule and untrained staff – half a dozen or so. Regardless of prices and incomes, the NBPI could have been profitably retained for independent investigative purposes. This aspect of the NBPI was, alas, entirely disregarded.

All that we are left with now is a Monopolies and Mergers Commission, based on a tenuous distinction between, on the one hand, the big and public, and therefore potentially baleful, and, on the other, the private rest, automatically deemed beneficent. This distinction flies in the face of all the reports of the NBPI and the Price Commission. They have pointed to an inefficiency which is universal to the British economy. It is to this that the CIM, thwarted by Mr Heath in an aberrant Selsdon phase, should have addressed itself. Let us in the next chapter indulge in an act of imagination and consider how it might have functioned.

[5]   *British Business*, 3 October 1980, p. 222.

14

HOW A COMMISSION FOR INDUSTRY AND MANPOWER MIGHT WORK

All Chancellors of the Exchequer written about in this book have been preoccupied with the problem of inflation, slight in the early post-war years and then accelerating. It is not clear why and how this inflation started.

> the monetarist solution ... traces inflation to a single cause, and there follows the apparently simple policy implication: get this single variable right and all else will follow ... The real world, however, is messy and muddled and, for me, the various pieces of the jigsaw contributed by the non-monetarists offer more insight into the causes of inflation than the simple monetarist model.[1]

I write with the same scepticism about the exclusively monetary cause of inflation. Simple monetarism, after all, was the lesson inculcated in youth, and with the passage of years the world has appeared more complicated. It is possible that the informed citizens emerging from the war on to the sunlit uplands of the welfare state had had their expectations raised high and that this was the precipitating cause of the inflation. Once started, the inflation was then kept going by the failure of managements adequately to control traditional incentives to effort as against the cry of employees for equity or comparability. Comparability in turn may have contributed to parallelism in prices. 'In industries in which labour costs rise as a result of negotiated wage increases ... Sellers will appreciate that all members of the group will have incurred an increase in costs, often a very similar increase. They will appreciate that if all sellers raise their prices in parallel the loss of sales may be small.'[2]

---

[1] M. Wilkinson, 'The New Inflation: Monetarist and Non-Monetarist Explanations of Recent Inflation in the U.K.', *Economics*, 16, Part 4, No. 72, Winter 1980.
[2] Monopolies Commission, Parallel Pricing, Cmnd. 5330, 1973, p. 36.

Conversely, parallelism in prices may have encouraged comparability in the determination of incomes. It is the reciprocity of action between incomes and prices which constitutes the case for a CIM looking, as did the NBPI, at both incomes and prices together. Prices in this context include profits, whether retained in the firm or distributed to shareholders. When profits go up, claims for increases in incomes (mainly wages) inevitably follow.

But is there a case for a CIM now? Yes there is, on three grounds. First, there is no neat distinction between the competitive and the monopolistic; the one fades insensibly into the other; all prices and incomes should therefore be open to be looked at, and not just so-called monopolistic ones. Secondly, there is a possible conflict of approach between that of the Monopolies and Mergers Commission and that of a body charged with supervising prices. Sir Arthur (now Lord) Cockfield, Chairman of the Price Commission, testified: 'the closer the functions of the Price Commission and of the Monopolies Commission become and [*sic*] the less justification there is for the maintenance of two separate bodies each trying to approach what is essentially the same problem with different, and potentially conflicting, rules and procedures. And, perhaps even more disturbing, each with a different approach and philosophy'.[3] Thirdly, even with an unemployment rate rising to 13 per cent, the index of labour costs per unit of manufacturing output rose from 100 in 1980 to 120 by the end of 1984[4] – hardly a case for no control. This is not a good augury for a favourable balance of payments when North Sea oil is exhausted.

The critical question is whether the CIM should be given a semblance of supreme authority or whether the British practice that only Parliament should bear apparent supremacy should be adhered to. When, in the United States, two separate boards were set up, one for pay and one for prices, the justification lay in the fact that the United States, used to quasi-regulatory agencies in a constitution divided between legislative, administrative and judicial functions, was not unaccustomed to this kind of animal. The 'agency' was a semi-legislative body. The United Kingdom, however, is different. Here Government or Parliament (choose which you will) reign supreme, and even the Price Commission, when it wished to change the code under which it operated, had to seek the Government's and perhaps Parliament's

---

[3]　Sir Arthur Cockfield, 'The Price Commission and the Price Control', *The Three Banks Review*, March 1978, No. 17.

[4]　Central Statistical Office, *Monthly Digest of Statistics*, No. 470, February 1985, HMSO, Table 7.3.

permission. Mr Heath, in copying the American model, had failed to appreciate the difference in the constitution of the two countries. The NBPI was always subject to the Government. Because of the publicity to which it gave rise prominent parliamentarians suspected it of subverting Parliament. The suspicion was entirely unfounded. Mr George Brown on one occasion sent an emissary in the shape of Sir Eric (now Lord) Roll, his Permanent Secretary, to beseech me to play down the publicity. I replied that the publicity was no doing of mine; it just arose. To me the constitutional position was clear: the Board made recommendations to the Government; whether the Government chose to act on them or not was entirely its own affair.

Since ultimate power then can reside in the United Kingdom only in the Government, the CIM or the Pay Board can be set up only by Government through Parliament. There was nonetheless, a fundamental distinction between the proposed CIM and the Pay Board. The decisions of the Pay Board were open to appeal before the courts of law. This made it difficult for the Pay Board to introduce a degree of flexibility into its judgements. Indeed I doubt whether a strict adherence to a tight code and a measure of flexibility can be combined. The NBPI, by contrast, acted in an advisory capacity to the Government. Its judgements could either be accepted or repudiated. This was a weakness. Equally, however, there was the gain of flexibility, which I would myself regard as an advantage. If the same practice were to hold for the CIM, which is what I would recommend, its terms of reference would be laid down by the Government. The CIM should, however, unlike the NBPI, be free to choose its own references. The criteria which the CIM should be asked to bear in mind should also be different from those to which the NBPI had to work. There should certainly be a 'norm' for incomes – probably the recent rather than the prospective rate of increase in output per man. The scope for increases above the norm should however, be more restricted than under the NBPI. The NBPI was empowered to give exceptional increases on the following grounds: where pay was low (and low pay is a relative, not an absolute, concept); where pay had fallen out of line or unduly behind (much the same thing); where there was a shortage of labour; and where there had been an increase in productivity. The last exception was grossly abused, not by the NBPI itself, but by employers and the Department of Employment, which was given the function, for which it was ill equipped, of scrutinising productivity schemes.

Of those grounds for an exceptional increase in pay I would retain mainly one – where there was a shortage of labour in specific grades which could not be remedied by training within the firm itself, or which could not be overcome by improving the efficiency of existing labour resources or by changing production methods. The vexed issue of productivity would be covered by these words. I would ensure that claims on the ground of improved productivity be strictly controlled, the controlling body being the CIM. For price increases, I would have only one criterion: namely, where, after every attempt had been made to reduce costs (including labour costs) an increase was necessary to finance new investment. Where a number of firms were shown to be practising parallel pricing, each could be looked at in turn in the light of this criterion. Given this criterion, there would be no purpose in looking at 'adminstered' prices, i.e. prices imposed by a seller on the market as distinct from competitive prices which have to be accepted from the market. The point would be covered.

The NBPI could not choose its own references; it was given them. And they fluctuated in number. When the Wilson Government toyed with the ideas contained in 'In Place of Strife', a document aimed at curtailing the power of the unions, the number of income references dropped steeply. As the election of 1970 approached the number of price references increased sharply.

This alternation, not between parties, but within one party, could not but be disadvantageous to the NBPI. A government has to make up its mind; either it seeks to control incomes directly or it seeks to do so indirectly through assailing the power of the unions. The attempt to do the latter under two Conservative Governments – 1979 to 1983 and that from 1983 onwards – has patently failed. '. . . inflationary pressure is still present despite over 3 m. unemployed and the union pay mark-up is higher in the 1980's than ever before in the post war period.'[5] While that failure continues, an incomes policy is far from being discredited.

As far as references were concerned, the NBPI might ask for a reference, as it did in the case of cars, but it was not always given. The pretext given for refusing cars was that a reference might upset the attempt to form for the car industry a special sub-committee of the National Economic Development Office. One was eventually formed, under the chairmanship, if I remember rightly, of a representative of the car industry; its report claimed for the industry a ridiculously high rate of return – 27 per cent, if my memory serves me. The Price Commission, by contrast with the NBPI, was allowed to choose its own

[5]   *Midland Bank Review*, Spring 1985, p. 15.

references. But it had to court Government Departments to make use of this freedom, and it was often shunted off.

There is in truth a close bond between a firm or an industry and the sponsoring Department. I had first noticed this at the Ministry of Fuel and Power. The Ministry derived most of its information on oil from the oil companies themselves, and when oil rationing was introduced Ministry and companies worked closely together. I came across the same phenomenon again at the NBPI, when dealing with bank charges. To a question why the clearing banks had not resorted to greater competition when exhorted to by Lord Cromer, then Governor of the Bank of England, Sir Archibald Forbes, then chairman of the Midland Bank, replied that they had conferred with Reggie Maudling, as Chancellor, and he had frowned upon the idea. Government Departments tend to throw a protective cloak around the sponsored firm or industry. To lift this cloak a Government Department should be under a compulsion to give reasons publicly why it wishes to refuse a reference asked for, unless the reasons contain a commercial secret. As a sequel to the NBPI's inquiry into bank charges, the Treasury refused to make a statement; they feared that the recommendations made might lead to a loss of control over the supply of money. Yet the recommendation of the Board – namely, that there should be greater competition between financial organisations – ultimately came about, and with no impairment of monetary control, in so far as that is possible. The Board saw more clearly ahead than did the Treasury, and the Treasury, had it been forced to give reasons, would have shown itself in the event to be short-sighted.

The NBPI had no sanction to help it enforce its recommendations, beyond a governmental power of delaying an increase in prices and incomes, the length of the delay varying from time to time. Its real power lay in the cogency of its conclusions, which employers and employees found it difficult to rebut. While still believing that the main influence on the actions of firms and unions is through argument, I would no longer consider the sanction of a delaying power strong enough. The sanction would need to be based on certain principles. It would need to be recognised, as was brought out in the last chapter, that the primary responsibility lay with management. It is against management therefore that the sanction should be directed. This sanction would come into play if management had conceded a pay increase without justification or equally unjustifiably had raised a price.

It has been suggested that a suitable sanction would be a tax on the firm. If, as I consider and both Keynes and Lord Cockfield considered, the economy be fundamentally monopolistic, there is no reason why the tax should not be passed on by the firm to the consumer by way of higher prices. Lord Cockfield, as quoted earlier, has been quite emphatic, 'One thing which clearly emerged from price control was the extent to which competition is effectively limited in this country.'[6] Since the object of the exercise would be to avert increases in prices, the particular sanction of a tax as a penalty for an 'excessive' wage, given Lord Cockfield's diagnosis, which coincides with mine, would be self-defeating.

The alternative is therefore a sanction aimed directly at preventing price increases. If more than its due share is paid out to labour in current income, the direct increase in prices which could result could be estopped. If equally, in the case of a reference on prices, the firm went ahead and raised its prices against a recommendation by the CIM the increase could again be estopped. The resources available to the firm would be diminished and thus indirectly its ability to distribute larger dividends. There would be no need for a direct restraint on dividend increases. Clearly the power of estopment can reside only in the Government, which can accept or ignore a recommendation of the CIM, as was the case under the NBPI.

There can thus be a power to stop certain wage and price increases, not as a substitute for, but as a complement to, the management of demand, no matter whether this is through the supply of money (and therefore roughly Friedmanite) or through the budget (and therefore roughly Keynesian).

The operation of a prices and incomes policy by a CIM would need, however, to be buttressed by other institutions, institutions which have been largely absent under previous prices and incomes policies. The institutions would be three: job evaluation in firms above a certain size; legal participation by workers in the taking of certain decisions; and, most difficult of all, the admission of workers into share ownership. The broad aim of all three institutions would be to abate the conflict between capital and labour and thus reduce the burden on a prices and incomes policy.

Job evaluation means the ranking of jobs in a hierarchy, the main criterion of a rank being to my mind the degree of responsibility or dis-

---

6   Cockfield, op. cit.

cretion exercised. The ranking requires that management and employees sit down together to determine the order in which jobs are placed. That is the begining of participation. Job evaluation is thus a means of introducing a sense of equity at least within the firm. Once that is established increases in pay should be in accord with the national policy. There has over the last decade been a considerable spread of job evaluation schemes, but since the Department of Employment no longer monitors developments in the private sector there is no official knowledge of their extent or nature. It could be a legal requirement therefore that all job evaluation schemes introduced in firms above a certain size be registered with the CIM. There would inevitably be differences betwen schemes, but the CIM could use its influence to try and ensure that schemes were based, as far as possible, on like principles. Such a likeness of principle is important for the determination of public service pay.

The Megaw Report on Civil Service Pay (1982) is the latest in a long series of inquiries, stretching back to the early years of the century, in concluding that civil service pay has inevitably to be based on some form of comparability with the private sector. Such comparability requires job evaluation schemes both in the civil service (and by extension, other parts of the public service) and in the private sector. The more closely alike are the schemes, the better founded can be the comparison. In spite of a recommendation by Megaw no job evaluation scheme has yet been framed for the Civil Service.

Participation in the taking of decisions is a natural extension of job evaluation. The purpose of participation should be the accretion of value added (that is, the difference between revenues and the costs of materials and services). There are three levels at which participation is relevant: the plant, the division (based on either a product or a region), and the company. There should be legislation prescribing for this arrangement. It is clearly participation at the level of the plant which interests the employee most. Participation at that level means that he is told of proposed plans for the plant, his views on them sought, and a decision taken in the light of his views. This does not necessarily mean the destruction of managerial prerogative in the plant; it means only that certain decisions should be joint.

The same holds for decisions at the higher levels of the division and the company. When the chairman of the National Coal Board invites the leader of the National Union of Mineworkers to discuss with him the future of the coal industry, he is doing more than just imparting information; he is also seeking a reaction to the information. The decision should be taken by the chairman in the light of the reaction. Participation cannot mean the surrender of the power of decision from the management to the employees; for that could mean, as it has meant in Yugoslavia, an emphasis on short-term considerations as against longer-term considerations, and that is no way to redress the relative decline of Britain.

In the next chapter I state the case for a two-tier board – an executive board and a supervisory board. It goes without saying that the employees, besides being represented on plant, divisional and company councils, as suggested in this chapter, would also be represented on the upper tier or supervisory board.

A third institutional reform which could conceivably buttress a prices and incomes policy is the spread among workers of share ownership. The virtue of this reform is that it could encourage employees to a tolerance of profits. Many schemes have been mooted, some have been tried, but in no Western capitalist society can the execution so far be said to have been crowned with success. The concept of shares for workers throws up a range or problems. Should the scheme be voluntary or compulsory? Should the shares be in the workers' own firm or should they be shares in a variety of other firms, through, for example, a unit trust? Should the number of shares allotted be equal for all workers or should they bear some relationship to the hierarchy of salaries within the firm? The primary consideration to be borne in mind in pondering these questions is whether the answer adds to the total volume of saving and investment or subtracts from it.[7]

In the light of this criterion my own answers to the questions posed would be as follow. The scheme should be compulsory rather than voluntary, it being an obligation on the firm to set aside a fixed proportion, say, 5 per cent, of its added value to be held in trust for its employees. If the scheme were voluntary rather than compulsory, if, that is, it were left to the employee to take up shares or not, there is a strong probability that he would prefer current income. The fund set aside by the firm should be deductible for tax purposes, though it has to be said in the case of the United Kingdom that not many companies pay large amounts of corporation tax. Equally, the employees' title to a share in the fund should be exempt from income tax, but should be

[7]   Carlo Casarosa, *Il Risparmio Contrattuale*, Aula Magna dell'Università Cattolica del S. Cuore, Milan, 1984.

subject to capital gains tax on sale, which should not be allowed for a certain number of years, say, five or seven. The remission of taxes both to the firm and its employees would, of course, be at the expense of the state and might therefore lead to a decline in saving and investment by the state. Further I should be in favour of the company's council's, on which employees would sit, investing in other firms, for this would make capital more mobile and not congeal it in a particular firm. Finally, in my view the distribution of shares should bear some relationship to the hierarchy of salaries, for equality of shares could be at the expense of saving.

Enough has been said to show that the question of share ownership by employees bristles with difficulties. A firm, for example, might seek to evade the imposition on it of a fund for employees by putting up prices. Equally, an employee might seek to evade what he might regard as forced saving by claiming a higher income. In either case the effect could be inflationary. For this reason a scheme for share ownership by employees has to be accompanied by a firm prices and incomes policy. The concept of employee share ownership cannot be judged in the abstract; each scheme has to be seen in its context, particularly, in the context of a concomitant prices and incomes policy.

There remains the further problem of the public service employee, whose work or contribution to value added cannot be measured. The device of investing his title to shares in a variety of companies would, however, place him on a par with an employee in the commercial sector. The one difference would be that the employees' shareholding could not be a percentage of value added – for this quantity is unknown. The sum of money set aside for shareholding by employees would therefore have to be arbitrarily determined. And its management would have to be subject to the same tight regard for the prices and incomes policy as the commercial sector.

In advocating employee shareholding I am aware of the likely difficulties, in particular the difficulty that the employee may be so conscious of his status as such that he might not wish to become a capitalist, that he would regard himself as joining the ranks of the 'enemy', and that at best he would reduce the allocation of shares to the level of collective bargaining. The fact is that in the United Kingdom employers and employees remain framed in a Marxist conflict; neither of them really wishes to break out of the inherited frame. This is the main obstacle to employee shareholding in the United

Kingdom. The proportion of the British working force owning shares is around only between 2 and 3 per cent. When, however, I contemplate the enthusiasm with which council house tenants have bought their houses and refurbished them, I spy a gleam of hope. After all, British society is undergoing a great transformation; share ownership by employees can and should be part of that transformation. And if brought about on a wide-enough scale it might encourage in the employee a tolerance of profits.

It was noted in Chapter 12 that there are two elements making for inflation – the level of demand and cost-push – that is, the striving of society for a degree of equity whatever the level of demand. The present chapter has been confined to the problem of cost-push. What, I trust, it has demonstrated is that the cost-push element in inflation requires more than a short-term prices and incomes policy; it requires widespread and difficult institutional reform.

15

THE VIEW FROM WITH-
IN BRITISH INDUSTRY

It has been demonostrated in the chapters on energy and aerospace that the private contractors to governments were careless of costs and inept at marketing. Are private firms not serving government any different? I have, in the interals between other preoccupations, been associated with a number of industries and companies – steel, fibres, machine tools, insurance, power tools, chemicals and the multifarious activities of a conglomerate. It would be invidious to refer to particular companies, except when the occasion makes it inevitable. What lessons, if any, have I derived from the experience, even though I know it not be representative?

The chapters on the public utilities – electricity and gas – described the presence of a multiplicity of undertakings, municipal and private, all of them being overtaken by a technology which required a degree of amalgamation. Either because they did not see the direction of technology or because they were unwilling to sink individual interests, they failed to come together and thus invited nationalisation. That indeed is the case for action by the state – to do that which private firms are unable or unwilling to do. Companies in the private sector of which I had a glimpse behaved no differently from the gas and electricity undertakings.

The steel industry, thanks to strong independent leadership, quickly recovered from the destruction of the Second World War and launched upon a series of expansion plans. But to the best of my knowledge the attempt to emulate the large integrated plants of Japan was belated. In any case it would have demanded some sinking of individual interests. There was none. On the advent of the Labour Government of 1964 I was asked to produce a paper setting out the reasons why the main steel interests of a particular company should not be nationalised. I accepted that this could be done, but that the argument would be fortified if the company showed a willingness to rationalise its activities with another company in the same area. Such rashness was disallowed, and the paper was all the feebler as a result. The same company owned an obsolete steelworks. The steel subsidiary purchased ground for the construction of a new plant. The parent Board, however, was averse from the risk.

Independence, which may or may not coincide with the maximisation of profits, is a company's principal aim. And independence means independence for the existing managements, not necessarily the welfare of the shareholders, though they in turn often form a loyalty to the company and identify themselves with continued independence. To secure independence a company seeks to grow big, and size is most easily obtained through the acquisition of other companies, either for cash or shares. If the acquisition is by shares the share price has to be maintained; for this reason there is a tendency to disperse profits rather than plough them back into the enterprise.

However large a company, it invariably falls upon an evil day, possibly for transitory reasons. The predator then pounces. The financial columns of the newspapers are filled with screaming headlines. Emotion rules the roost and detachment is suspect because it is a contradiction of loyalty. The most emotional scene I witnessed was at Courtaulds, when ICI made a bid for the shares. And when the battle was over a church service was held thanking the Lord for delivery from the hands of ICI. I did not attend.

I mention Courtaulds because Mr D. C. Coleman, in his history of the company,[1] singles out my name as the one director who, at the decisive meeting, voted in favour of accepting the ICI bid. That is quite true, and while I was the only one to vote I was not the only one to hold my view. My view was based on the fact that Courtaulds had a monopoly in the oldest man-made fibre – viscose, but had only just begun to penetrate the newer field of synthetic fibres. If the company was to move forward it could do so only by acquiring a decaying textile industry and so safeguard for itself an outlet for viscose. If, equally, it moved increasingly into synthetic fibres it would be entering a field where there was looming excess capacity. It was precisely in these two directions that the company subsequently moved, and while profits may now look shining they can remain so only if the primary dependence on viscose has been removed.

'Ah', but I was told, 'the valuation which I.C.I. put on the shares is too low; our share price should be higher.' I still wonder how shares

---

[1]   D. C. Coleman, *Courtaulds: An Economic & Social History*, Vol. III, *Crisis and Change 1940–1965*, Clarendon Press, Oxford, 1980.

are valued. The valuation can scarcely be based on the long-term prospects of the company, for these are veiled from operators on the Stock Exchange and often from the company directors. They can only bear some relationship to the profits of other companies as known or guessed. '... the information available to the stock market is very imperfect.'[2]

Hence the tactics during a take-over battle of raising the estimate of profits. This is achieved by cutting such things as the depreciation provision to cover the decay of capital equipment and expenditure on research and development, and so adding a short-term hope to the existing shareholder, but also undermining the future profitability of the company and therefore the future prospects for shareholders. Actual profits are invariably compared month by month with budgeted profits. On one occasion actual proftis for a particular month were well down compared with the budget. The manager in charge explained that the month in question had been a holiday month. I pointed out that we were concerned with the difference between the outcome and the budget. The fact that the month had contained a holiday was of relevance only if the budget were drawn up for an entire year and divided by twelve. This was not, however, the case. The budget was an estimate for the month in question and thus already took into account the fact of a holiday. The explanation given the Board for the low profits thus did not hold. I do not believe that the manager was trying to deceive the board; I believe he was just confused. If this kind of confusion can enter into explanations given to a Board, how much greater is the possible confusion concealed in statements to shareholders when a potential take-over is being fought off!

Profits can, of course, improve over time as compared with the budget. But the improvement is seldom, if ever, suddenly dramatic. At first it is tentative and one is never sure how long it will last. Hence my scepticism about long-range profit forecasts in a take-over battle.

Even when the battle is over and a rescuer has appeared in the shape of a lender or a sharer in the equity he is seldom told the truth about the profit outlook. One such company in receipt of aid had a plant which was in such a mess that one particular form of consultants I knew refused to help put it right. To the creditor, however, who asked what progress was being made with the plant the chief executive

[2]   J. G. Tulip Meeks and G. Meeks, 'The Case for a Tougher Merger Policy', *Fiscal Studies*, July 1981.

replied that it would be some little time yet before the plant could be said to be earning 10 per cent on the investment. It was then making heavy losses. The truth can also be concealed from the Board itself. In this particular instance the plant manager was asked his estimate of when the plant might break even. He replied that he did not know. Either he did not know or, in order to protect himself, he chose to conceal his estimate.

A chief executive, particularly when fortified by executives and non-executives who have spent a lifetime with the company, can play an important part in the choice of chairman. Normally he will want a malleable chairman. I have known a retiring chairman succumb to the chief executive's wishes and announce his successor at short notice, leaving no time for more independent members of the board to seek an alternative candidate.

Similarly I have seen a chief executive choose his finance director without regard to the wishes of others. The finance director in question came from within the company. Certain of the non-executive directors were fearful lest he be too subservient to the chief executive. They accordingly suggested that the vacancy be advertised. Every time an application appeared in response to the advertisement the internal candidate was summoned to the chief executive's presence and instructed to amend his own application to make it more comparable with applications from the outside. The internal candidate was duly appointed. I doubt whether any of the other non-executive directors had the faintest idea of what had happened.

When a company is in difficulties, temporary or permanent, one recourse open to a non-executive is to seek the intercession of the Investors' Protection Committee. There was one occasion on which I did this. The response was to refer me to the merchant bank, which, of course had a permanent relationship with the company, no matter whether it was doing indifferently or well. I got nowhere.

In short, the permanency of a board of directors is represented by its executive members, and not by its non-executives. Non-executive members are sometimes recruited from the ranks of former executives. They are then victims of the same blind loyalty as executives themselves. They do not have the open-mindedness which a non-executive director should have. One may well ask how the salaries of executive members are determined. In the case of one company the chief executive, doubtless in concert with his executive colleagues, laid down guidelines for the determination of managerial salaries in subsidiaries. These guidelines were never submitted to the Board as a whole. Once, however, salaries in subsidiaries had been settled, the chief executive would come along to the non-executive members of the main board and seek increases of x, y or z for his executive colleagues. In this way a platform was erected for the settlement of his own salary by non-executive members who knew nothing of the preceding events. They generally based their answer on a vague idea of comparability with other companies, but without undertaking any proper study.

Nor were non-executives in my experience able to influence executive members of the Board towards a fuller degree of participation in decision-making by workers. When the Bullock Committee on Industrial Democracy was set up in 1976, a questionnaire was circulated to companies about their practices and intentions. One company replied that it was consulting a great deal. In vain did I point out that the answer evaded the question, which was concerned with the participation of workers in the taking of decisions. Nothing was ever changed. Indeed I have scarcely ever heard personnel matters discussed around a board table. The most might be a report by whichever director had been entrusted with the part-time job of concerning himself with personnel to the effect that a wage claim had been received by the relevant employers' organisation. The rest of the board would nod sagely, encouraging him to resistance. Unions might have to be tolerated, but were mistrusted. No credit was ever to be given to them, and there was no sense of the reciprocal obligation between employer and employee which obtains in Japan.

Equally defective I found corporate planning. Planning to me, represents an attempt to picture over time likely changes in technology and markets together with a sketch of the adaptation contemplated on the part of the company. The corporate planning which I saw consisted of an estimate of the funds available to the firm over time, either generated by itself or by borrowing by one means or another, and the resulting scope for acquisitions, with the aim of establishing size. This was an accounting exercise, not a plan. But the bleating voice of a non-executive had no effect.

A company which specialises in the purchase and sale of other companies is a conglomerate. Its theoretical justification is that only through belonging to a 'mother' company can the subsidiaries obtain the capital needed for their development. With financial help and a degree of managerial guidance the subsidiaries proceed in their own way. The 'mother' company then prides itself on practising a policy of decentralisation, and decentralisation is held to be the embodiment of efficiency. The other side of the coin, however, can be flawed. The expertise at the centre is too thin fully to comprehend the wide spectrum of activities under its shelter; it has difficulty in maintaining a balance between them, and in the attempt to keep balance it can stultify the development of some of the larger subsidiaries; more particularly, it lacks the width of knowledge to judge adequately investment in totally new fields and as a result sometimes comes a cropper; finally, since its business is the buying and selling of companies it is not interested in new products and in the research and development required for their birth. R and D is judged to be too risky and marketing is left to the subsidiaries. I have seldom known the board of a British, as distinct from an American, company to contain either a technical or a marketing specialist.

By contrast, the best company that I was ever associated with was concerned with products and their selling. It was American in parentage, and the marketing was excellent. One doubt which I entertained was about the technology, the expenditure on R and D being no greater than in an average company – at most 2 per cent of turnover, most of it being done in the United States; the R and D done in Europe amounted to only 1 per cent of turnover. Like most American companies it did not allow unions. Yet the organisation was such that the head of a plant ate in the same canteen as the ordinary employees. Through a hierarchy of circles stretching downwards reasonably full information was transmitted from the top to the bottom. Thus there was information and up to a point consultation, but scarcely participation.

A frequently used ratio was that of indirect labour to direct labour. An increase in this ratio was deemed bad. Yet, as research and development expands, as computerisation is introduced, the ratio of indirect (mainly staff) to direct labour increases. For this reason I considered that the company was adhering to an out-of-date formula.

It is easier for an American than for a British company to make a donation to a political party. In the case of a British company some 70 per cent of the shares are held by institutions – insurance companies and pension funds. One can argue that one does not know the political wishes of actual or potential recipients of pensions or of those taking out insurance policies. As for the 30 per cent individual shareholders most, if not all, would probably be Conservative. There is a good case for maintaining therefore that the company should make no political donation. This is not so with the United Kingdom subsidiary of an American company. The wishes of the shareholder – the American parent – are clearly expressed; it likes to give financial support to the Conservative Party. The Conservative Party has much to gain from the presence in this country of subsidiaries of companies in the United States.

The main question raised by the descriptions in this chapter is the relationship between executive and non-executive members of a board. The board as a whole is nominally accountable to the shareholders, but the annual general meeting of shareholders is normally a farce. The odd question may be asked, but it is generally wide of the mark. In the upshot the board is accountable to nobody, unless perchance disaster befalls. Further, the co-existence on the same board of executive and non-executive members certainly makes for a greater understanding by the latter; but it also makes for a degree of intimacy between the two sets of directors which helps to soften the criticism of the outsider. Indeed I have known of a case where the chief executive has sought to get rid of a non-executive member because of his questioning. For these two reasons – the absence of accountability by a board, and the intimacy which can develop on a board between executives and non-executives – I am in favour of a two-tier board structure. Only through his presence on an upper-tier board can a non-executive director hope to push his point through.

The main requirement on an upper-tier board is critical and independent-minded directors. This is so whether they are representatives nominated by the shareholders, which in the main would be the institutions or representatives nominated by the workers, whether they are shareholders or not. It would be preferable for the firm's workers to nominate directors outside their own ranks. I am well aware of the criticism normally levelled against such an arrangement – namely, that secret conclaves arise between executives. They do anyhow, even now under a unitary board. At the unitary board meeting the ordinary executive member is silent, leaving the expression of the collective voice to the chief executive, even though an individual director may disagree with it. Provided the inquiries launched by the upper-tier board were persistent and relentless enough, they should act as a spur to the management which both the Prices and Incomes Board and myself in my personal experience have identified as the main weakness of British industry. I should add the view that the two-tier structure should be legislated for, for in easy-going Britain little change is accomplished without legislation.

I have so far spoken of companies and not of associations of companies. The main association is, of course, the CBI. I was familiar with it in its former guise of the FBI (Federation of British Industries), being for a while a member of its panel on economic affairs. The transformation into the CBI was an enlargement, the new body bringing in the British Employers' Confederation and a string of smaller companies. Possibly because of the enlargement the CBI was biased towards the Conservative Party. Although it had signed the Statement of Intent, it influenced the brewers into a reluctance to disclose profit figures when the NBPI was required to investigate brewers' prices. Across the table of the National Economic Development Council (Neddy) the late Mr George Woodcock, when General Secretary of the TUC, used to taunt the late Mr John Davies, Director General of the CBI and later a Conservative Minister, about the fact that the TUC had set up a committee to vet wage claims, while the CBI had done nothing. Subsequently, when John Davies had given way to Sir Campbell Adamson, the boot was on the other foot. The CBI influenced at any rate some firms into freezing prices, while the TUC, to the best of my knowledge, did nothing. CBI and TUC confronted each other in exactly the same way as the political parties. While ostensibly industrial, the CBI is in its heart of hearts, a political organisation. This is regrettable, for the credibility of its industrial advice is thereby undermined. But then the CBI merely holds up the mirror to its constituent firms. The weakness of the National Economic Development Council is that it imitates the House of Commons. The two representative organisations sit opposite each other, just as do the two main parties in the House of Commons. They address each other as political parties and the still, objective voice is seldom heard.

My experience of industry both preceded and followed my spell at the NBPI. The lesson borne in on me at the NBPI was one of pervasive optimism and inefficiency. But for the rare exception I cannot say that my direct experience of industry contradicted that lesson. Conservative governments in particular can scarcely conceal their admiration for the private sector. No doubt good appointments can be made from that sector. But in general governments should beware. The management of British industry in general, like that of American industry, is no more than average.

16

THE THATCHERITE COUNTER-REVOLUTION

There is no disagreement that the United Kingdom was the first country to embark on an industrial revolution and that the revolution's apogee was symbolised by the Crystal Palace Exhibition of 1851. There is equally no disagreement that there has been a decline in Britain's relative status as an industrial country. There is some disagreement over the date at which the decline began. Some place it before 1851, some after. The exact date, however, does not matter; what matters is the indisputable fact of relative decline. I have suggested that the relative decline may now be turning into an absolute one, so great has been the destruction of equipment and the demoralisation of the workforce.

Various explanations of the decline have been put forward. Some ascribe the decline to the absorption of the industrialist by the preceding culture, though why this should have occurred in Britain and not elsewhere is not clear.[1] Others attribute it to the educational system, not in the sense that part has been public and part private, but in the sense that in both cases the purpose of education was to befit a person to be a good Christian and not necessarily adept at the business of living.[2] Yet others explain the change by an over-long attachment to under-developed colonial markets and, as a result, the continued production of out-of-date goods.[3] Then there are those for whom the answer is to be found in the prolonged existence in a stable society of semi-monopolistic organisations gathering to themselves as much of

---

[1] Wiener, *English Culture and the Decline of the Industrial Spirits, 1850–90*, Cambridge University Press, 1981.
[2] Barnett, *The Collapse of British Power*, Eyre Methuen, London, 1972.
[3] Kirby, *The Decline of British Economic Power since 1870*, Allen and Unwin, London, 1981.

133

the national product as they could.[4] This explanation leaves out of account the possible collaboration, tacit or explicit, between different semi-monopolistic organisations. Finally, and more recently, there is Pollard,[5] whose basic explanation is lack of investment, due in the main to attempts by Government to contain inflation by depressing demand.

There may be something in each of these explanations, and they each may go some way towards explaining in particular Britain's evolution in the nineteenth century. My own concern in this book has been with Britain in the century in which I have lived – the twentieth, during which in Western countries the political constitution has been based on representative democracy, a factor of great importance, for it means that all individuals are politically equal. Economically the dominating feature of this century has been the occurrence of two deep depressions, possibly with different causes and certainly with different remedies to right them. The first depression, during which I grew to adulthood in one of the worst areas of unemployment, took place despite low interest rates and was accompanied by a collapse of consumption.[6] Its persistence was explained by Keynes as due to lack of purchasing power, in spite of 'sticky' wages, to buy the goods which could potentially have been produced. His remedy was to complement the deficiency in purchasing power through specific expenditure, particularly on investment, by the state. The failure of Keynesianism was that no amount of extra domestic purchasing power could offset the rising unemployment in so far as this was due to a growing lack of competitiveness in international trade; public spending could remedy unemployment in the domestic field only, and not in the field having to cope with the rest of the world. After the Second World War, for whatever reason, further unemployment was, at any rate for a time, indeed averted; but at the same time, whether or not due to the expectation of full employment, or to the fact that institutions had failed to adapt themselves to the Keynesian intellectual revolution, there appeared an inflation, slight at first, but accelerating. Possible causes of the inflation other than Keynesianism have been seen in this book – in particular, an optimism and excess of ambition on the morrow of a

[4]   Olson, *The Rise and Decline of Nations*, Yale University Press, 1982.
[5]   Pollard, *The Wasting of the British Economy*, Croom Helm, London, 1982.
[6]   Peter Temin, *Did Monetary Forces cause the Great Depression?*, Norton, New York, 1976.

triumphant war, in aerospace and in newly nationalised industries such as coal and electricity, and correspondingly a heightened degree of expectation in the community at large.

The first and most important cause of the current depression, which started before Mrs Thatcher, had been the invasion of markets previously served by the United Kingdom by newly industrialising countries, particularly from South East Asia and, to an extent, Brazil. The thesis has been advanced that Britain, due to an over-reliance on colonial markets, had exported out-of-date goods and had had to import more up-to-date products; this observation was confirmed by the initial experience of the Ministry of Technology, which observed that we were exporting less-sophisticated and importing more-sophisticated goods. The propensity to import was also the subject of several letters sent out by Mr Macmillan in the early 1960s. The failure of the Keynesian prescription to maintain employment through an expansionary Budget was due primarily to the propensity to import; had we lived in a closed economy Keynesianism could have maintained full employment. The rise of South East Asia, as a competitor to British exporters, has been graphically described by Mr Brian Reading.

> Today the E.E.C. has contracted to 93 per cent of American's GNP and the Pacific 10 [20 major Pacific-basin economies] have expanded to 62 per cent. From less than half of us they have grown to two-thirds our size. They will easily overtake us before this century is over. The economic centre of gravity of the free world is moving from mid-Atlantic to mid-Pacific.[7]

To the relative decline of the post-war period, which was but a resumption of the relative decline which had preceded the Second World War, Mrs Thatcher, coming to office in 1979, reacted with a counter-revolutionary view. It would be foolish to express a final judgement on the counter-revolution after a mere five years, though such a judgement has been expressed on the five-year period of the National Board for Prices and Incomes and the shorter phases of other forms of incomes policy. There are, however, certain indicative signs.

The counter-revolutionary thesis appeared to contain the following elements: a belief that the inflation was due to one cause and one cause only – an excess of money: the corresponding belief that the Govern-

[7] Brian Reading, *The Sunday Times*, 5 February 1984.

ment could exercise a sovereign role over the supply of money through a flexible rate of exchange, thus rendering it independent of any other country's policy; a determination to restore the 'right' of management to manage rather than surrender to such ideals as worker participation; a resolve that in the intervals between elections Government should be sovereign, without any obligation 'to consult or negotiate with anyone else'.[8]

Each of these elements may be examined in turn. First, the belief that the entire blame for inflation was to be laid on an excess of money. The only apparent symptoms of an excess of money were high wage claims, which could have been attributed to other causes, and a slight deficit in the balance of payments, which at that stage could be covered by borrowing from overseas. In the budget of 1979 the rate of growth in the supply of money as then defined was set at 7–11 per cent, a figure which, according to intention, was to decline to 4–8 per cent by 1983–4. Prices nonetheless rose, partly because of higher wages, partly because of higher indirect taxes. The supply of money then accommodated itself to the higher wages and prices. As a result 'the credibility of the targets was destroyed when they were substantially exceeded for each of the first three years'.[9] The targets were then raised and the definitions of the supply of money began to multiply. The monetarist explanation of the British plight thus became discredited. Certainly it could not have accounted for the relative decline of the British economy for over a century.

The attempt to curb the excess of money was pursued both through a tight monetary policy (high interest rates) and reduced Government spending, the opposite of the policy followed in the United States, where, alongside a tight supply of money, Government spent lavishly. The high rates of interest required by the monetary policy, which reached an all-time record of 17 per cent in November 1979, in turn raised the exchange rate, already high by virtue of the fact that sterling was now a petro-currency.

The high rate of exchange, while it may have helped the Government to abate inflation through the lower price of imported goods, worsened the balance of payments in manufactures, as seen in table 4.

---

[8]   David Cobham, *The Three Banks Review*, No. 143, September 1984.
[9]   Brian Reddaway, 'Problems and Prospects for the UK Economy', *Economic Record*, September 1983.

Table 4 *Balance of payments in manufactures (£m)*

	Exports	Imports	Visible balance
1980	34,818	31,177	3,641
1981	34,639	31,993	2,646
1982	37,313	37,114	199
1983	39,919	44,905	−4,986

Over the period January 1984–November 1984 inclusive the visible balance for each month (seasonally adjusted) was consistently negative.
Source: Central Statistical office, *Monthly Digest of Statistics*, No. 469, January 1985, Table 15.1.

It thus aggravated the problem of the imbalance between the export of lower-grade goods as against the import of higher-grade goods.

Nor is there any likelihood that this imbalance will be redressed through investment. The importance of investment is that it foretells the future. A failure to invest today will mean a poor tomorrow. Interest rates throughout 1983 hovered between 11 and 9 per cent, and around 9 per cent in 1984. These high real rates of interest of 5–7 per cent have adversely affected investment in manufacturing industry, as shown in table 5.

After more than five years there was no sign of any increase in investment to the level of 1979.

Nor, to take the second element in Mrs Thatcher's counter-revolutionary policy, has she been able to assert sovereignty over the supply of money through a flexible exchange rate. High interest rates in the United States pulled money towards that country, made it difficult to reduce them in the United Kingdom and upheld the British exchange rate.

The United Kingdom, as a result of the monetary policy, was first into the recession and went in much more deeply than other OECD countries. The attempt to remedy the national problem through a tighter control of the supply of money had in fact aggravated it. Tardily there was some recognition of this. From early 1982 onwards the exchange value of the pound began to decline. This was due in part to

Table 5 *Fixed capital expenditure in manufacturing industry (£m)*

Revalued at 1980 prices	
1978	7220
1979	7496
1980	6471
1981	4852
1982	4685
1983	4619
1984	5257 (provisional)

Source: Central Statistical Office, *Monthly Digest of Statistics*, No. 470, February 1985, HMSO, Table 1.8.

the fall in the price of oil, in part to the competitive difficulties faced by British manufacturing industry as a result of the highly valued pound, and in part to the outflow of capital which has constantly continued since the abolition of controls on capital in 1979. The depreciating pound threatened, however, the Government's policy of eliminating inflation, and in 1983 there was substantial intervention by the Bank of England to moderate the pace of depreciation.

But, will it not be said, have not Mrs Thatcher's policies resulted in improved 'productivity'? To this question several answers can be advanced. First, oil output, which first appeared under Mrs Thatcher, was accompanied by little use of labour; this fact alone would have caused 'productivity' in industry and mining to rise. Secondly, as far as productivity in industry alone is concerned, the recession would have caused companies to close down their worst plants and keep in operation their best; on this score again productivity would have risen. By the same token, however, a recovery will require new plants, and these cannot be quickly brought into being. Thirdly, 'productivity' is a vague concept, in that it fails to take into account the changing composition of output – for example, the substitution of products embodying new technology for those embodying old technology. By this criterion the introduction of robots into manufacturing industries has been slower in the United Kingdom than elsewhere. Lastly, 'productivity', defined as output per man, rose between 1979 and 1984 by roughly 9 per cent. The increase in labour productivity was natural, given that, with increasing unemployment, the ratio of capital to labour rose.

More important than productivity, however, is the trend in labour costs per unit of output. On indices based on 1980 = 100, earnings in manufacturing had risen by the end of 1984 to 155.1, while labour costs per unit of output had risen to 120. The rise was aggravated while the foreign exchange value of the pound was also rising, thus worsening our competitive condition, the peak being reached in 1981; a decline took place as the pound subsequently declined. Even so the British competitive position was worse in mid-1984 than in 1978 – 86.6 as against 68.1 on the IMF Index (1980 = 100).

It is frequently said that high wages cause unemployment. This is not so. It is high labour costs per unit of output relatively to other countries which bring in their train a lack of international competitiveness and with it unemployment. And relatively high unit labour costs may in turn be due to inferior technology.

Cannot employment, it may be said, be found in the service industries? The decline in manufacturing employment is known; the likely demand for service employment is shrouded in darkness. In the decade 1970–80 employment in manufacturing in the United Kingdom declined by 1.4 million, or 18 per cent of all employees in the manufacturing sector, and in the four years 1980–4 by a further 1.4 million (22 per cent). These are worse figures than anything that occurred in the United States. The U.S. Bureau of Labour Statistics has, however, made an estimate of the likely increase in service employment between 1982 and 1995. The average increase is expected to be around 25 per cent of the much larger United States working force, mainly in hospitals and local government. Such an increase in the United Kingdom would not be enough to offset the decline in manufacturing employment – 40 per cent of the working force – which has taken place since 1970. The answer to unemployment does not therefore lie in the services sector.

The third element in the counter-revolutionary philosophy listed at the outset of this chapter has been a desire to restore to management the right to manage. This desire is adduced as one of the reasons for the Government's aversion from an incomes policy. '. . . incomes policies to be effective . . . require trade union acceptance, and the attempt to gain such acceptance involves the government in a process of negotiation in which its right to be the sole policy-maker is diluted and compromised.'[10] Our political constitution is that of a representative democracy; democracy is not something which suddenly emerges

[10] David Cobham, op. cit., p. 28.

every five years or so; it requires a constant interchange of views between economic agents and the government of the day.

Grievances can arise among democratic equals when some of no apparently greater merit appear to be doing better. No one wants complete equality. But in a small island where everybody is politically equal to his neighbour there is a limit to the degree of economic inequality which is tolerated. It is the struggle for the acceptable degree of inequality which goes under the name of 'comparability'. It is not the fact that trade unions are monopolies which makes for cost-push; there are equally strong monopolies on the other side. Wage increases are easily passed on into prices, the monopolistic behaviour of companies matching that of unions. Both sets of monopolies, however, are impelled by the same motive – the attainment of a near-parity with their compeers.

It is this which results in cost-push, a problem which Mrs Thatcher does not believe to exist. Various institutional changes have been suggested in this book for mitigating the problem – in particular, the ranking of jobs primarily according to responsibility exercised, the extension to workers of a degree of participation in decisions, and the admission of workers to share-ownership, all as auxiliary to a prices and incomes policy designed to deal with cost-push, including wages and most prices. In contrast to these suggested reforms managements have reacted to the recession by saying in effect: 'We are the masters now.' If we ever emerge from the recession that attitude is likely to bring its retribution. Democracy in politics cannot but result in an attempted extension into economics; to deny this is to fail to see that democracy evolves and is plainly reactionary.

The same comment holds for the fourth strand in the counter-revolutionary thesis – namely, that in the intervals of authority Government should be sovereign, not needing 'to consult or negotiate with any one else'. Such an attitude diminishes a government's awareness of a nation's feelings and simply makes for bad government. Not only has the expression 'elected dictatorship' become a description; what is worse is that it is an avowed aim.

On the political side then the counter-revolution runs against trends which have been developing for some decades and for this reason seems destined to ultimate defeat. On the economic side there has been a modification of the monetarist view; none of us now is a monetarist in the original sense that too much money was the sole source of all evil. In its place there has been greater prominence for an associated thesis – that all blame attaches to the public sector, while the private sector is apparently blameless. This book has, I trust, shown conclusively that there is no foundation to this thesis either. Nationalisation came about because the private or municipal undertakings which preceded the nationalised corporations were unable or unwilling to sink their differences; further, nationalisation made possible an effort in research and development which had been utterly neglected. As far as the private aircraft industry was concerned it was lax in its costs (part of it indeed sought nationalisation) and myopic in its view of the world market. The investigations of the NBPI and the Price Commission have shown that the primary fault has lain with management rather than unions, that it is weakness in management which has failed to control costs and thus contributed to inflation. Further, the weakness in management has applied to both the public and the private sectors. Yet it is to unions rather than to managements that Mrs Thatcher has directed her attention. The relative decline of Britain, above all, the tendency to import goods of higher value and export goods of lower value, is a national rather than a sectional weakness, and is due basically to a failure to translate inventiveness into marketable goods and a failure in marketing itself. It has nothing to do with the distinction between the public and private sectors. The main problem is that, because of long association with the Commonwealth, we tend to export inferior goods and to import superior ones.

I do not consider that the present level of unemployment is the product of faster technological change. True, the pace of technological change can be only doubtfully measured. For the last 40 years there has been technological change. There have been introduced the jet engine, the wide-bodied aircraft, the 'sputnik', the satellite, the computer, colour television and now cable television, etc. Nor is it proven that new technology reduces employment. One of the technologically most advanced countries is Japan, with a low unemployment rate. Since she is able to export high technology, employment is maintained. The Japanese example reinforces the point that Britain has been exporting inferior technology; hence the beginnings of the unemployment. Britain may be among the forefront in computer software programming, but to export she has to maintain a lead. Having seen so many older industries irrevocably and perhaps needlessly destroyed, she has now no option but to embrace new technologies if she is to recover anything approaching her lost industrial status.

There are various ways in which new technologies may be

introduced: multi-national companies may be encouraged to enter the country, bringing with them more up-to-date technology. There are in fact no formal barriers to their entry, though sometimes there is a mercantile insistence that components be made in the UK. Since the abolition of exchange controls in 1979, the net flow of capital has been constantly outward. True, a firm investing in, say, the United States may repatriate some of the technology learned there. Nonetheless, the outward flow is sufficiently impressive as to suggest that it has gone in search of a higher return. The figures are shown in table 6.

A statistical analysis of the Thatcherite years is given in Appendix 2. What this analysis shows is that, while the productivity of labour has increased, that of capital has declined and with it that of all factors of production.

If there is no great inward flow of technology, then a larger onus rests on the Government. What can it do? It may direct; or it may leave it all to the private sector. The Conservative Government rejects central direction, rightly, for no one can currently foretell the future. It should equally reject leaving it all to the private sector, for the private sector is immersed in the present, is averse from risk, and seeks a quick in preference to a delayed profit. The answer lies in co-operation between Government and private sector, if only because two heads are better than one.

What form should this co-operation take? There should be a futures unit, scanning social, market and technological trends, and their possible outcomes. The best location for such a unit, now that the Central Policy Review Staff has been mistakenly abolished, would probably be the British Technology Group, advised by ACARD. The Group should discuss its conclusions with industry, not endeavouring to coerce it, but certainly trying to convince it of the rightness of its thinking. If its thinking is accepted it should be ready to help financially, with research, development and procurement. The funds normally devoted by a firm to research and development are small; they should therefore be supplemented by Government help, either by grant or by loan.

Government financial help normally stops at the development or, at any rate the prototype stage, it being considered that the private sector would thereafter willingly buy. This does not necessarily follow, the purchase by Government or semi-Government organisations should form part of the entire package of Government help. I had once hoped that the procurement arm of the Ministry of Defence would play an

Table 6 *Total investment and other capital transactions ($£m$)*

1979	1834
1980	−1450
1981	−7353
1982	−3187
1983	−3648

Source: CSO, UK Balance of Payments, 1984 edn; HMSO Table 8.1.

important role in stimulating technology; certainly it appears to have done so in the United States. Defence institutions in the United States place research contracts for purposes wider than just the military, whereas in this country defence has given aid only to limited sectors – for example, aerospace.

The most important bodies after the Ministry of Defence are the nationalised industries. The National Coal Board, for example, has played an important part in promoting mining technology. No conscious effort has been made by Government, however, to use the nationalised industries to this end. For this reason, among others, I would regard their break-up as retrograde. Finally, there is the international dimension. Collaboration with others in aerospace has been technically successful; but nuclear power apart, I should be hard put to it to cite another instance where it has even been attempted. One of the purposes of our continued presence in the European Economic Community should be to co-operate with European countries in research and development.

What is happening at the moment is that the members of the Community, acting as independent sovereign states, try to form their own technological links with either the United States or Japan. They thus jeopardise the prospects for European technology, and thus eventually for each European country.

It is possible that co-operation between Government and private industry in the manner described might put an end to the fruitless controversy between the public and the private domains. It is this controversy which is associated with the division in politics; reciprocally the political divide exacerbates the controversy through constant alternation of policy; this makes impossible both continuity and any lasting reform of the capitalist system. The concepts at the root of the controversy – pure Socialism and pure private enterprise – are dead. Other countries have crept up on us through 'planning by dialogue'. It is there, in collaboration between the public and private sectors, that the future lies.

APPENDIX 1

A Ministry of Technology Memorandum to Harold Macmillan, Prime Minister, 30 December 1957

Sir Norman Brook has mentioned to me that part of his report to you on defence organisation which suggests a Ministry of Science and Technology, and I should like, if I may, to express my own personal views on this matter.

Our economic prosperity depends largely upon our ability to develop new products and to apply a high degree of skill to limited quantities of raw materials. Adequate technological development is, however, unlikely without some measure of Government push, and governmental arrangements for looking after technological matters seem to me in certain respects defective.

Governmental responsibility in technology is divided into separate watertight compartments. On the defence side, where the overwhelming bulk of public expenditure on research and development takes place, responsibility lies with the Ministry of Supply and the Admiralty. On the civil side, the Department of Scientific and Industrial Research, and the Medical and Agricultural Research Councils answer to the Lord President's office. (In addition individual Departments such as the Ministry of Power have their scientific sections.) This dichotomy between defence and civil scientific work contrasts markedly with the Russian arrangement, in which both are integrated in the Academy of Sciences, the Academy apportioning research, defence and civil, over a wide range of scientific establishments . . . It contrasts also with the unitary nature of technology, where no hard and fast line between defence and civil can be drawn. It means that defence scientific establishments are used hardly at all for civil purposes, though it would represent a saving in scientific facilities so to use them; and that the practical expertise, e.g., in placing and monitoring development contracts, which has been acquired in the defence field is scarcely used in the civil field. Finally, it renders difficult a solution to the problem which I ventured to bring before the Cabinet last July (5 CC(57)51st) and which I still believe to be a real one:

namely that the compression in defence scientific effort will not be automatically offset by an increase in civil scientific effort and that in the event trained men will be lost to the service of technology in this country.

I conclude that it is desirable to have within Government a centre linking defence and civil technology, and endeavouring to aim research to practical ends. This centre is best built round the Ministry of Supply, both because of the sheer preponderance and the practical character of the defence technological effort which it undertakes. The suggestion sometimes made, that the Ministry of Supply should either be absorbed in the Ministry of Defence or redispersed among the Service Departments, would effectively block all possibility of advancing technology outwards from the inner core of defence work, and would for this and many other reasons be, in my judgment, a retrograde step.

I am not suggesting that there should be any intrusion of Government into the academic (i.e. university) side of research; I have no special knowledge of this and from all I hear I believe it to be well done. Nor am I suggesting that individual Departments such as the Ministry of Power should lose their scientific sections; I am suggesting rather that there should be a Department of State charged with the task of co-ordinating technological work over its whole range and with seeing that the promising ideas are carried to the practical development stage. I am equally not suggesting the disruption of the Department of Scientific and Industrial Research. The theme is integration, not disruption, and the initial appropriate step would be to bring under a single Minister the scientific work of the Ministry of Supply and the Department of Scientific and Inudstrial Research, the latter remaining for the time being as now organised. The attachment of some other Government scientific agencies, e.g. those under the Admiralty, would undoubtedly have to follow later. I would not envisage any change in the arrangements by which the Ministry of Supply now does scientific work for the Service Departments. Since, however, the new Department would need to concentrate on technology, some procurement functions outside the scientific field would be inappropriate to it and could revert to the Service Departments. There would be many difficult questions of frontier demarcation to be examined, but I should make this letter far too long if I attempted to cover every aspect of the problem. I am, however, at your disposal if you wish to discuss further either the general idea or some of its detailed implications.

APPENDIX 2

The Statistical Record (UK): 1979–83 (Index numbers, 1979 = 100)

	Share of gross profits in GDP	Labour productivity (a)	Capital productivity (b)	Capital/labour ratio (c)	Total factor input (d)	Total factor productivity (e)
1979	32.4	100.00	100.00	100.00	100.00	100.00
1980	31.1	97.87	94.70	103.35	100.24	96.85
1981	31.7	101.05	91.36	110.61	99.99	95.45
1982	33.5	105.02	91.37	114.94	100.74	96.66
1983	34.5	109.40	92.12	118.76	101.68	98.54

Notes: (a) Gross Domestic Product ÷ number of employees
(b) Gross Domestic Product ÷ gross capital stock
(c) Gross capital stock ÷ number of employees
(d) Weighted average of the input of capital and labour
(e) Gross Domestic Product ÷ total factor input

APPENDIX 3

The contribution of different fuels to the energy demand of different countries

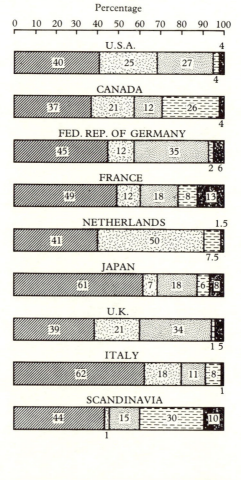

Percentage

U.S.A. — Oil 40, Natural gas 25, Solid fuels 27, Water power 4, Nuclear 4

CANADA — Oil 37, Natural gas 21, Solid fuels 12, Water power 26, Nuclear 4

FED. REP. OF GERMANY — Oil 45, Natural gas 12, Solid fuels 35, Water power 2, Nuclear 6

FRANCE — Oil 49, Natural gas 12, Solid fuels 18, Water power 8, Nuclear 13

NETHERLANDS — Oil 41, Natural gas 50, Water power 1.5, Nuclear 7.5

JAPAN — Oil 61, Natural gas 7, Solid fuels 18, Water power 6, Nuclear 8

U.K. — Oil 39, Natural gas 21, Solid fuels 34, Water power 1, Nuclear 5

ITALY — Oil 62, Natural gas 18, Solid fuels 11, Water power 8, Nuclear 1

SCANDINAVIA — Oil 44, Natural gas 1, Solid fuels 15, Water power 30, Nuclear 10

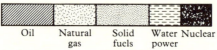

Oil   Natural   Solid   Water   Nuclear
      gas   fuels   power

NATIONAL DEMAND BY FUEL
1982

SELECT
BIBLIOGRAPHY

Albert and R. J. Ball, *Towards European Recovery in the 1980s*, European Parliament Working Documents, 1983.

Corelli Barnett, *The Collapse of British Power*, Eyre Methuen, London, 1972.

Earl of Birkenhead, *The Prof in Two Worlds*, Collins, London, 1961.

Carlo Casarola, *Il Risparmio Contrattuale*, Aula Magna dell'Università Cattolica del S. Cuore, Milan, 1984.

Carlo M. Cippola, ed., *The Economic Decline of Empires*, Methuen, London, 1970.

D. C. Coleman, *Courtaulds: An Economic and Social History*, Vol. III, Clarendon Press, Oxford, 1980.

P. Lesley Cook and A. J. Surrey, *Energy Policy*, Martin Robertson, London, 1977.

J. C. R. Dow, *The Management of the British Economy 1945–60*, Cambridge University Press, 1965.

Wolf Häfele, *Energy in a Finite World*, Ballinger, Cambridge, Mass, 1981.

Leslie Hannah, *Electricity before Nationalisation*, Macmillan, London, 1979.

M. W. Kirby, *The Decline of British Economic Power since 1870*, Allen and Unwin, London, 1981.

Ralph Landaü, *Technology, Economics and Policies*, National Academy of Engineering, Washington DC, 1982.

David S. Landes, *The Unbound Prometheus*, Cambridge University Press, 1969.

P. Lesley Cook and A. J. Surrey, *Energy Policy*, Martin Robertson, London, 1977.

R. C. O. Matthews, C. H. Feinstein and J. C. Odling-Smee, *British Economic Growth 1856–1973*, Stanford University Press, 1982.

Mancur Olson, *The Rise and Decline of Nations*, Yale University Press, New Haven, 1982.

Sidney Pollard, *The Wasting of the British Economy*, Croom Helm, London, 1982.

Michael V. Posner, *Fuel Policy*, Macmillan, London, 1973.

S. J. Prais, *Productivity and Industrial Structure*, Cambridge University Press, 1981.

Richard Pryke, *Public Enterprise in Practice*, MacGibbon and Kee, London, 1979.

The Nationalised Industries, Policies and Performance since 1968, Martin Robertson, Oxford 1981.

Josef Rembser, *The Need for Re-industrialisation – Industrial Policy in the Federal Republic of Germany*, Tällberg Workshop, Sweden, May 1982.

Peter Temin, *Did Monetary Forces cause the Great Depression?*, Norton, New York, 1976.

Martin J. Wiener, *English Culture and the Decline of the Industrial Spirits, 1850–90*, Cambridge University Press, 1981.

Trevor I Williams, *A History of the British Gas Industry*, Oxford University Press, 1981.

Williams, Williams and Thomas, *Why are the British Bad at Manufacturing?* Routledge and Keegan Paul, London, 1983.

INDEX

Adamson, Sir Campbell, 132
Advanced Gas Cooled Reactor (AGR), 45, 48, 69
Advisory Council for Applied Research and Development (ACARD), 88, 90, 93, 142
Agence Française pour la Maîtrise de l'Energie, 21–2
Agence Nationale pour la Valorisation de la Recherche (ANVAR), 90
Agriculture, Ministry of, 106, 110–11
Air Ministry, 73, 74
Airbus, European, 81
aircraft industry, 71–82, 93, 141; and international co-operation, 80–1
Alcan Ltd, 103
Alfa-Laval, 93
Algeria, import of gas from, 53, 55, 57
Amory, Lord, see Heathcoat-Amory, Derick
Anglo-Iranian Oil Company, nationalisation of, 58
Armstrong, Sir William, 114
Arnold, Dr Thomas, 4
Atomic Energy Authority (AEA), 39, 41, 42, 46, 48
Avro 748 aircraft, 77–8

back-benchers, influence of, 13–14, 15–16
balance of payments, 10, 12, 14, 95, 96, 98, 136–7
bank charges, NBPI inquiry into, 119
Barnett, Corelli, 4, 5
Benn, Anthony Wedgwood, 38, 87
Bennett, Sir Peter, 9
Benson, Henry, Lord, 79
Berkely nuclear reactor, 45
Bevin, Ernest, 9
Birch, Nigel, 12

Birmingham, immigration issues in, 16, 17–18
Blackett, Patrick, 86
Blue Streak missile, 73–5
boards of companies, 122, 128–9, 130, 131–2
Bowman, Sir James, 31
Boyle, Sir Dermot, 59
Boyle, Sir Edward, 18, 24
Bradwell nuclear reactor, 45
Brewers' Society, 104, 132
Briggs, Professor Asa, 101
Bristol Aero-Engines Ltd, 74
British Aerospace, 81
British Airways, privatisation of, 81, 82
British Electricity Authority, 36; see also Central Electricity Authority
British Employers' Confederation, 132
British European Airways (BEA), 75–6, 77
British Nationality Act (1948), 17
British Nuclear Fuels, 48–9
British Overseas Airways Corporation (BOAC), 75, 79
British Oxygen Corporation, 103
British Petroleum (BP), 58
British Technology Group, 89, 90, 93, 142
Bronowski, Dr J., 39
Brook, Sir Norman (later Lord Norman-Brook), 85, 89, 145
Brown, George Alfred (later Lord George-Brown), 96, 97, 98–9, 117
Brundrett, Sir Frederick, 74
Budget, budgetary methods of economic control, 10, 94, 95, 120
building societies, 106
Bullock Committee on Industrial Democracy, 129
Bundesministerium für Forschung und Technologie (BMFT), 90–1